Retreat
to the Finger Lakes

EXPLORING THE FINGER LAKES
FOR REST, RELAXATION AND RENEWAL

by Leona Jensen

Retreat to the Finger Lakes

ISBN # 0-9624738-3-9

published by
CHAPEL STREET
PUBLISHING

Dedicated to

the women in my life

who are unafraid to be themselves,

and to the guardians

of the Finger Lakes.

TABLE OF CONTENTS

PREFACE

Most of the activities in this book occur annually near the end of July unless otherwise stated. In the back of the book is a list of some sources of information on many subjects about the Central Finger Lakes region. It includes Indian lore on how the Finger Lakes were made by the Great Spirit when he rested his hand on the earth, Sullivan's famous campaign, fish trophies, grape growers that produce "the best" wines, origins of Women's Rights, tour, canoe and hiking information and many interesting items about the Finger Lakes region.

Leona Jensen
Penn Yan, New York
June, 1992

WANDERLUST

There is a need which every housewife with children has felt when the endless details and pressures of daily living become overwhelming: the need to be alone - absolutely alone-to recharge and renew the spirit. Not meeting this need in some form is a contributing factor to many unhappy marriages, although it is not purely a need of women. Men in our society have always been able to "get away" more easily than women. There have been recent signs of progress: women are finding themselves able to follow paths and interests not normally accepted a few years ago.

Determined not to let my own opportunity pass, I planned a retreat for myself. Alone.

Not being born to wealth, I found certain constraints to my wanderlust. It could not cost over a hundred dollars. I began to look closely at my own backyard.

The Finger Lakes region is one of the richest in four season natural beauty, least life threatening places in the world. The water is clean, the air is relatively pure and crisp, and there are few insects, mammals or reptiles that might inflict a serious wound if encountered accidentally. The people are trustworthy and friendly, although somewhat reserved. The weather on the whole is mild, with seasons that highlight the rolling hills, blue lakes and mysterious gorges. It seemed an ideal place for my retreat, so I took a closer look.

The history of the people and geology of the Finger Lakes is rich. Six hundred million years ago, before there were plants on land, this area was the bottom of a tropical sea. Salt deposits from that sea are now mined where that ancient body of water served as the playground for the trilobite, a beetle-like bottom feeder that grew to about four inches in length and whose imprints are treasured by fossil hunters who come here from all over the world.

As millions of years passed there were great upheavels of the earth and great storms. Ponderous ice sheets crushed and scoured the land. When the ice melted, the land was scarred with gorges and piles of debris were deposited by rushing waters released from the icy plows.

In more millions of years, Native Americans from primative nomads to the highly developed Iroqouis Confederacy camped along the Finger Lakes waterways. Their fire circles and arrowheads are scattered across the land and around the lakes. Their lives were finely tuned to the ebb and flow of nature. Today, it is easy to experience the vague feeling of company as you walk the trails and fields. You can almost see their spirits sifting through the woods as a morning fog swirls from the valleys, or catch a glimpse of their shadows among the trees as the golden harvest moonbeams glance off flaming yellow and red leaves. In their turn, those leaves slip from the branches to blanket the ground and return their minerals to what the Indians thought of as their Mother, the Earth.

My closer look at this region filled me with greater expectation for my retreat.

The State of New York recognizes that it has "places-without-price" and has established public parks to hold them in trust for everyone's enjoyment. For a few dollars, and with very little equipment or the most modern of campers, anyone can stay in the State Parks and numerous smaller county parks. It is a two edged sword. It is no small feat to preserve the natural beauty and survive the onslaught of thousands of visitors at the same time.

A variety of activities are available to visitors: swimming, lectures on local flora and fauna, volleyball, horseshoe courts, nature trails, hiking and ski trails, and museums. Best of all are the shadow-throwing campfires with toasted marshmallows and fellowship.

My mind had visited the imagined peaceful places long before it was time to get my equipment ready, and it was difficult not to be anxious. I was offered all kinds of advice for planning easy nutritious meals to backpack for six days. The provisions I came up with consisted mostly of dried foods from the grocery shelves that either only needed water for cooking, or could be eaten as is. The food was repacked into bags labeled breakfast, lunch, dinner, snacks, condiments and drinks.

Gradually I assembled my equipment while in the process of trying to find items which members of the family had borrowed. The essential items were hidden in the corner of the bedroom to keep them from being "borrowed" back.

I planned an orderly departure, and on the long-awaited day when my generous husband and children went their way and I prepared to go mine, I was the last to leave the house. I found myself frantically throwing the remaining perishables from the refrigerator into the cooler, fearful of returning to a refrigerator that was greener than the forests I was seeking out. I had all the goodies which were too "good" to throw away.

It was not until all of my painstakingly assembled equipment was in the back of the van in a disorganized heap that I remembered my oversize, saddle-basketed bike had to be loaded too. It would fit. I would make it fit.

Still, I had to make the inevitable trips back into the house for the last minute packing essentials like maps, recharged flashlight, and a gallon of drinking water. At last I locked the house door in the ninety-five degree heat and began to question the sanity of this Retreat. Dripping with perspiration and filled with anticipation, I mentally went over my list while starting the van, said, "now or never", and scooted quickly before friend Murphy had a chance to knock. Murphy's Law number 77: "Plans with the greatest desire are proportionally most likely to be interrupted, or conversely, the dentist never cancels appointments."

And so I invite you to join me on my adventures around the Finger Lakes.

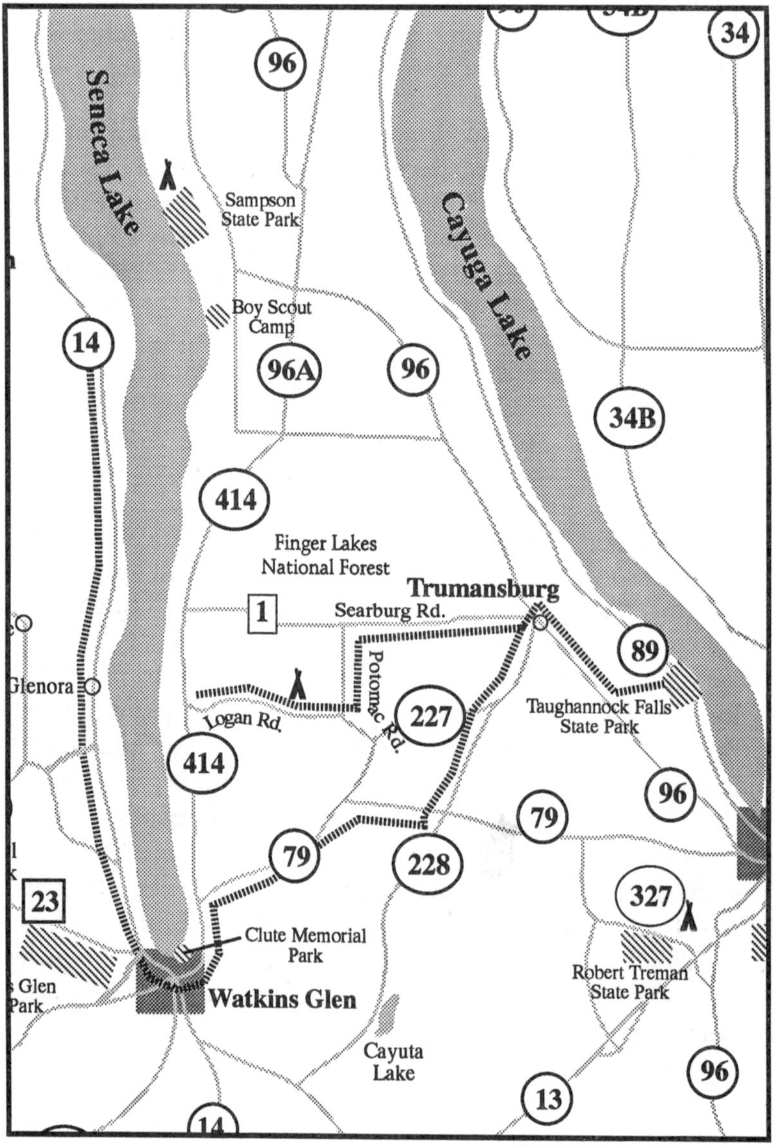
Seneca Lake
Cayuga Lake
Sampson State Park
Boy Scout Camp
Finger Lakes National Forest
Trumansburg
Searburg Rd.
Potomac Rd.
Logan Rd.
Glenora
Taughannock Falls State Park
Clute Memorial Park
Watkins Glen
Cayuta Lake
Robert Treman State Park
96
34
14
96A
34B
414
1
89
227
79
228
327
23
13

RETREAT

I should escape far away and find a refuge in the wilderness;
soon I should find myself a sanctuary from wind and storm,
from the blasts of calumny,
O Lord, from my enemies' contentious tongues.

Psalm 55 vs. 7-9

It is said that even the longest journey starts with but a single step... well, here I go! Heading toward the highway I put away nagging thoughts like, do you really want to go by yourself? The whole family can visit relatives almost anytime and the "me" in I is ready. This is one chance for my spirit to wander with tumbling waters. I'll be better able to meet obligations if I go than if I don't, so go it is.

Gaining momentum, the air blowing in the window, second thoughts are forgotten as I head south on Route 14 along the west side of Seneca Lake. With wind flipping my hair, and the deep greens of a summer afternoon guiding the concrete highway, I feel I could drive forever. I look at the land as if for the first time, savoring the cedar speckled fallow fields and the vineyard's tidy rows of grapes slipping down the hillside to the lightly ruffled blue-green waters of the lake. What an expansive view! Where else can you see a lake as it melts into either horizon and still see its opposite shore looking like a toy model countryside?

The green sentinel red cedars seem to prefer the land between the lakes. The red heart wood repels insects and the outer shaggy, shedding bark makes a good fire starter. The aromatic evergreen has two kinds of leaves, sharp awl shaped and flat rounded leaves. The dense growth around the main trunk makes it a favorite nesting place for birds. Cedar trees are slow growing because they are usually growing in poor soil. They cannot tolerate full shade and as the fallow fields go through the stages of succession and golden rod and briars are replaced by maples and oaks, the lower branches die until there is only a cap of green struggling for the available light. Then one day their rib-like skeletons fall, often caught and leaning upon the very tree whose shade killed them.

On down Route 14, stark square cement shafts of the largest and deepest salt mine stand as bleak monuments to the stunted fields around them. Morton Salt started construction in 1969 and closed the mine in 1976. They claimed the reason for closing was a decrease in the demand for road salt - a win for the roadside and downstream environment.

Since then all kinds of uses have been proposed for the land and its salty chambers. Storage of crude oil and nuclear waste was proposed. Now there is a park and public boat launch site by the lake where the pumping station was that pumped water up the hill to dissolve the waste salt. A giant hill of millions of tons of waste salt was dissolved and pumped back into wells 1,400 feet deep.

The short monetary gains did not balance the salt's effects on the topside environment. Blowing salt dust either killed or stunted the immediate surrounding farmland while the mine digging contaminated some local water wells. Although the mine is closed, it's effects will linger for a long while.

A few miles to the west in a gentle valley is the small village of Dundee. It was started like many villages in the Finger Lakes Region, from a saw mill utilizing the water power of a stream. The whole village of Dundee was nearly destroyed by two different fires in 1859 and 1860.

The future of Dundee might have been much different if certain influential people had not objected to the influx of dirty over-all'd railroad workers when New York Central Railroad wanted to build a railroad center in Dundee.

In the early 1900's it was the blackberry capital of the country. When chemical dyes took the market away during World War I there were enough other kinds of farms established that Dundee was able to survive as a small agriculture town. Now it is home to Seneca Foods, a large grape and fruit processing plant which is a subsidiary of S. S. Pierce, now owned by Kraft, a large food processor.

Dundee, besides being the first school district in New York State to centralize, is also the proud home of the well known Dundee Steel Drum Band. The Caribbean flavored music is made by hitting precisely dented and tuned steel drums.

Further down Route 14 is a small pollen colored, family operated honey stand, "Wixon's" where you can watch industrious bees make their hive and store their honey behind a glass window. A honey bee's short lifetime of hard labor produces one ounce of sweet honey. The honey's color and flavor is determined by the kinds of flowers visited.

Across the way from Wixon is Lakemont's Lakeview Freedom Village. Operated by a religious organization out of Rochester, it gives displaced teenagers another start as a substitute home. The buildings at Lakemont have been a seminary, an academy, and a retirement complex before becoming the much needed Freedom Village.

Next, route 14 crosses two of many steep gullies that characteristically cut the Finger Lakes hillsides: picturesque if you aren't afraid to look down through the whizzing far spaced steel railings on the barely two-lane narrow bridges.

Down the road in a farmland setting, overlooking the lake, is the location of the annual free Glenora Music and Arts Festival. People come from all over to enjoy the outdoor concert and art exhibits. On the corner, is the Glenora Winery, one of many offering tours and tastings. There are more than 89 superb wineries in the Finger Lakes Region.

Since New York passed a law allowing the establishment of home wineries with a limit of fifty thousand gallons of wine, many vinyardists have turned to making their own wine to ensure a market for their carefully tended flavorful grapes. There is a new guide book called *Wineries Of The Finger Lakes* that lists all the wineries and directions to them. Main roads have signs with a grape cluster to indicate nearby wineries.

Today is a picture book setting as white wakes trail behind tiny motor boats inching their way over the inviting blue water of Seneca Lake. The captains may be looking for a different place to fish or going back to a cozy cottage after an all day excursion, or water skiing session. Further down the forty mile long lake a half-dozen white sails dot the large expanse of water as they race diagonally, cutting the endless waves that appear as small ripples moving up the lake pushed by the wind.

Off in the rolling hills, about seven miles to the west below the small lakes of Waneta and Lamoka, is a hilltop state park called Sugar Hill Recreation Area. On its highest point is a fire tower where you can sit on the steps with a cup of coffee and watch a new day begin. If you are quick, awake, and don't blink, you can see the green flash phenomenon that happens just as the sun's first rays pass through the atmosphere. My early rising husband has seen it while we were on our yearly camp out at the park. We were attending one of the world famous archery contests held there, besides numerous archery courses.

Sugar Hill has horse, snowmobile, and cross country ski trails. The Finger Lakes Trail winds its way east through Sugar Hill on the way to Watkins Glen State Park. The name came from the time early settlers combined their efforts and held community sugar gathering "bees" in April. The numerous sugar maples provided ten to twelve gallons of sap per tree. Forty to fifty gallons of sap were boiled down to make one gallon of syrup. Records say that Brigham Young, an early founder of the Church of Latter Day Saints (Mormons) was one of the young workers who helped to collect the amber syrup in the early spring days long ago.

Traveling down the long descending road past the turn off that goes to the Irelandville Museum, to the head of Seneca Lake, you can barely see the Native American Symbols on the sheer rock cliffs on the eastern side of the lake. They are said to mark the Seneca's homeland and are near where the Senecas made a final valiant stand against Sullivan's Artillery, sent to rid the area of protesting Native Americans and make it safe for invading colonists.

Scenic Route 14 gently dips down into Watkins Glen nestled at the end of Seneca Lake. At the water's edge is a tour boat for taking rides on the lake, a long boardwalk dock and a miniature golf course. Next to the waterfront park at the edge of the business center is the Seneca Market place. It is a small seasonal shopping mall developed in and around old mill buildings and the tour boat ride dock.

The outdoor center square is reminiscent of European squares with brightly colored awnings, colorful flowers, heaped up wares, and tables and chairs. It is an inviting place to wander and relax with a cool glass of lemonade or New York Wine. But today, the goal is a peaceful place. Too bad, the people at the cafe tables look like they are having summertime fun.

The Route 14 signs point south on Main street. Some street signs are made in the shape of the first racing cars because the Grand Prix Races were once held on the Glen's streets. The frequently televised races have moved to a track out of town. The fast growing Racing Museum may be moving off the main street if they can find a larger building.

The state highway continues past the entrance of the 800 acre Watkins Glen State Park and the new laser light show called Timespell. The nineteen tumbling falls rushing through the twisting rock crevasse presents a new breathtaking view at each turn, especially if you climb the trail. Officially opened in 1863, it is famous for its rugged beauty and has been called the 8th Wonder of the World.

Whether you hike the twisting gorge trail or not, you can see the Timespell light show on the rocks nightly from May through November. The gorge is not open in the winter and early spring, but the cross country trails are. The song Big Rock Candy Mountain was inspired here years ago at a now forbidden swimming hole.

Instead of staying on Route 14, parts of which follow an old Native American trail and continues through Elmira to Penn-

sylvania, I turn left on Route 414 and head east around the end of Seneca Lake. This road takes me past the large building complex of the International Salt Company. To mine the salt here, wells are drilled into the ground and water is pumped down into the wells. The salt is dissolved and the brine is pumped back up and then the water is evaporated out.

As the road curves around the end of the lake, it suddenly becomes congested. There are people wandering back and forth across the road from the camping area of Clute Memorial Park on the right to the large tree-lined picnic area and swimming beach on the left. Boat trailers, like water striders are parked everywhere. On the beach - clustered like insects and colored like butterflies - are boats that look like they came from the south seas.

The two-hulled Catamaran sailing races are today! The row of beached Catamaran sails gently flap to and fro in the breeze as the captains and crew formulate last minute strategies for the exciting race.

I can almost feel the pull of the ropes as the sails tighten with the wind. First the water slips, then gurgles past the smooth hull as the power surge from the wind presses you back until you are one with the wind.

***

Excited clatter and chatter blur and fade as the van turns and climbs steeply up the opposite side of Seneca, over the dying Native Americans' pictorial statement. The sun's blinding reflections off the water ends my view of the racing fleet.

I lumber up the hill, which has turned to a cliff. At the crest, Seneca looks untouchable again. A sharp "Y" to the right on Route 79 eventually brings the van into shady cool greens, contemplation and small rural villages.

Now moving east between lakes, I proceed roller coaster style over mounds of glacial debris left millions of years ago. Up hill and down, not high, not wide, perfect roller coaster size at 55 miles per hour. One roll after another, past red barned farms, ripening cornfields, old and new houses, fallow fields and through shady woods.

Time for a nice cooling ice cream on a stick at a corner Mom & Pop store complete with gas, newspapers and a telephone. It seems to be out in the middle of nowhere, but busy none-the-less. There is a sign that says, Firewood For Sale, a sure summer sign that a state park is in the vicinity. Heavily used parks are generally scoured clean of story-telling and song-singing size firewood.

The chocolate covering begins to drip before half of the cold sweet cream is gone. The pleasure of its coldness is lost by frantic gobbling to eat it before it becomes a chocolate dribbling mess in my hands.

I decide to follow a sign that says Trumansburg this-a-way. It shouldn't be more than five miles, I guess, to Taughannock State Park on Cayuga Lake. Phooey, I turn off too soon and end up in Trumansburg, and so went a couple of miles 'round in a circle. Because I went too far north, I just have to back-track on Route 96. Before going far I find myself right in the middle of a traffic jam for the popular Annual Antique Car Show. The Trumansburg Fair Grounds are packed with rows of cars in the fields and long tents. Scores of people are carefully inspecting the rows of mirror polished and lovingly restored old cars.

The highway is lined with spectators' cars and traffic is stop-and-go until well past the fair grounds. I wonder if they have a hot dog stand? It looks like there is an entrance fee and brochure, an exhibition like this is much more fun when there is someone to explain to you what it is all about. So...on to Taughannock (Ta-can-ik) State Park.

Finally! There is a small sign pointing to the park. The road turns left toward Cayuga Lake and winds snake-like, following a nearly dry stream. The road forks and one fork goes over a bridge, so I stop hoping to get a nice picture of the falls. It's a disappointment: there are no falls here, just a barely-flowing stream, stepping down little stone stairs and disappearing into the woods. There are barely two inches of water flowing over a 100 foot flat, lightly rust colored, smooth slate bed. A small ankle deep pool below the bridge has captivated some children splashing other waders.

Is this the falls¿, I wonder, as two teenage boys watch me maneuver the van out of the awkward parking place and into traffic. I'm sure they are wondering if I will make it without taking part of the stone bridge, or another car with me. Disappointed in the falls, I'll look for a place to camp and take a quick swim in Cayuga Lake.

Not far down the road, toward the lake is a large practically deserted parking lot. It has the usual wooden barricades and a picnic area off to the side. Naturally I have to see what is here. As I explore a stone fenced path off to the side, an animated man heavily laden with box and camera is making video pictures of his family as they climb up the stone stairs.

Wow! A half mile or so in the distance is a high narrow falls cutting through the rock and crashing into a crater below. The specks I think are rocks are people standing by the thirty foot deep pool at the bottom of the two hundred and fifteen foot (higher than Niagara) falls. Dressed in shorts and sandals, I don't feel ready to venture down the trail to the pool just yet. But I put joining those insignificant specks at the foot of those falls high on my priority list.

On down the road toward Cayuga Lake, I plan. First I'll get a campsite, then go for a swim, and save exploring for later when it is cooler. The road goes through the campsite area with small circular roads angling off from the main winding road. Small brown signs say the office is down at the lake. Most of the sites look like they are occupied, but past experience has shown that many people leave on Sunday, so there should be some openings by now - right¿ - wrong!

After what seems to be endless twisting, the road reaches the bottom of the hill and intersects with a main highway, Route 89 from Ithaca. The office is across the street, but there is a city of people coming and going at the large beach and recreation area.

A stream also intersects the highway here but it has resumed its old character, not giving the least hint of the violent falls above. The road is lined with parked cars and there is a line waiting to pull into the park. The reason for so many people is that this is one of their famous "Sunday in the Park" concerts and I have arrived just in time to attend. The Park has a year-round, wide variety of programs and music.

I did not have a concert in mind for today, so on to the hiking destination, Blueberry Hill. Which means going back up the hill to Trumansburg and consulting the map for the best route west.

Settling in on the road, aiming the van in the right direction, a routine gauge check indicates the gas gauge is registering nearly empty. I should have filled up in Watkins, or where I stopped to check the map. Since Blueberry Hill, (part of the Hector Land Use Area, recently renamed the Finger Lakes National Forest) is about 8 miles due west from Trumansburg. I can stop on the way for gas.

The Hector Land Use Area was made part of the Green Mountains Park System to keep it from being sold to settle part of the National Debt and from being used to settle part of the Indian Land Claim. The claim would give thousands of acres and money to the Native Americans because of an illegal default in a treaty made and not ratified years ago.

The Blueberry Hill Campsite is located in the center of the Finger Lakes National Forest which is on a high ridge separating Seneca and Cayuga Lakes.

Up a long, steep hill into the blazing blinding sun: westward ho! The highway turns into a wide dirt and gravel road, dust billows out around and behind the van and up through the vents.

A small brown park sign points south to a smaller dirt road that disappears into the distance. It must go somewhere because here comes a car in a cloud of dust. I can't get lost between these two lakes high up on a hill, right?

The narrow road becomes rougher and dustier. There are signs along the road, on the edge of large fields, that say Public Grazing Land. When the woods start, the signs stop. I go slowly, partly to enjoy the scenery and partly to keep the dust from being unbearable, but mainly to be able to read any signs for directions to Blueberry Hill.

Now there are "No Hunting" signs. Pulling off the road, I consult the bicycle touring map, it shows that the Forest Land boundaries zig and zag all over, so this part must be on private land. Next, there are small park signs that show trails and paths on either side of the road. In the middle of nowhere a wide dirt road "t's" to the west. Blueberry Hill must be close: either that or I've missed it. I'll turn west and see if the campsite is this-a-way, the map says it is on an east/west road. Better get there soon, or find a gas station, or I won't be going anywhere.

At the crest of the hill there are more trail signs and a couple of pull offs into the thick woods for parking. Then the gravel road yardsticks straight off down the high hill toward Seneca Lake. Woods and fields are checkered on either side of the clay colored dusty road.

Now what? I must have missed the park or maybe it is down the hill further. Down, down, down, leaving a trail of dust hanging in the air. It's not steep, but my ears feel like I must be going down into the salt mines. Finally the road becomes paved and the fields populated with houses and trailers. Someplace around here is a camping area and an office. Down the hill some more and there's the main road, Route 414. The road I took from Watkins! No wonder I feel like I've been going in circles: I have! The map shows a park on the lake down the road, perhaps that is where the office is.

Down, down, down some more. Now the road is VERY steep, very narrow and twisting. Oh, what have I done? There has to be a turn-around here some place. My ears pop. The gas gauge is on the back of empty and that's with the van pointing down hill. Just as I round a sharp curve the road ends in a fork and I have to make a decision which way to turn. One fork is barely a driveway that ends in the lake, the other narrows still further and curves off along a steep bank into a private campground with a chain fence and a sign that says "Authorized Vehicles Only".

A small building is perched on the bank over-looking the water, so I squeeze the van off the road on a narrow band of grass next to a steep drop-off to the water.

Now the perspiration is from nerves, the van wheels are on the edge, its almost out of gas, I can't find the park, I'm sticking to the seat, I've been going in circles and I don't see anyone to ask for directions. It's a relief to find the camp store-office door open and the manager in.

"Blueberry Hill? I used to take horses up there and ride the trails. Haven't been up there in a few years. As far as I can remember, there's a bulletin board or something near the road at the campsite. The camp's back in the woods a-ways."

"Do you have any information on the trails?"

"Used to have some, but you can get maps and stuff at the Park Ranger Station back that-a-way in Odessa on Route 224," he says, sweeping his hand to the south.

***

If I had gone further into Watkins and taken the next road east, I would have gone right by the Ranger Station. Oh well, when I finally got a map of the Forest Land later, I found out they aren't open on Sundays.

Next question and most important, "Is there a gas station around here?"

"Yup, just go back up this road to the highway, turn left and it is a short way towards Valois" he explains, swinging his arm in the other direction to make sure I understand.

Fingers crossed and being careful not to use too much gas, I turn the van around and labor noisily up the seemingly endless twisting hill. My heart skipping every time the engine pings. The gauge is clearly beyond the empty mark and I keep looking ahead for nonexistent places to pull off the snaking road if the engine dies. The heat and discomfort are forgotten as I strain with the engine to inch the van up the hill. Once on the flat highway, hopes rise that the van might make it to a gas station. It takes forever for the oasis gas signs to creep around the bend in the road. It is such a relief to make it to the pump, that the high price of seven gallons is gladly paid and dutifully recorded, my second expense.

Now to continue the search for the elusive Blueberry Hill Campsite and the Finger Lakes Trail. Enjoying the scenery again now that transportation is assured.

It would be fun to ride horseback here, but according to the manager at the camp store, he doesn't know of any horses for rent in this area. A secret lifelong dream is to wander the woods on some noble steed. Mentally I relive the short excursions horseback riding while in high school as the van climbs the long, dusty hill.

Our horseback riding adventures were before liability and traffic became problems. We were able to ride through town streets and woods to an abandoned sand race track. Four of us would have about thirty minutes of the hour's rental time left to gallop around the race track, usually just once because the horses would veer off on the path that went back to the barn like they were on rubber bands. In our group,a high rating of horsemanship was given to the person who could get their steed to go around the track twice. Three times was unbelievable and made the ride back to the barn extra fast, as the horses had some inner clock that allowed them to tell when the hour was up.

As my motorized green steed bounced over bumps, clattering and splattering stones over the road, with dust rolling in the windows and up the vents, I moved horseback riding up on my list of things to do. Up, up, into the clouds of dust to the far reaching hills again, creeping along like a green bug on a prairie path. Near the top: aha, a dumpster! How could I have missed that tell tale sign of a camping area?

I rein into the parking lot, funnel into a hidden driveway, creep past an open pipe gate and into the woods. I have arrived, hiking here I come! Twice around the circle, slowly, first to pick out a campsite, then to dismount.

There are picnic tables, standing charcoal burners and fire

circles at each lot. The campsites are set back into the woods and are a fair distance from one another.

There are two little freshly painted outhouses on one side of the large circle, and a water spigot near the entrance gate. Registration is by the honor system according to the poster by the entrance. There are fifteen sites, and only two are occupied with tents. There doesn't seem to be anyone around anywhere. I pick a site that sets far back into the woods far away from the other sites, and back the van in.

Silence presses in after the noisy whooshing of the wind and clattering gravel. As my ears adjust, I can hear birds twittering in the trees overhead. On the ground there is a gentle breeze, but the tops of the trees are swishing roughly. Now I can hear someone at the rear of one of the other campsites 'mocking' wood. Chunck, wock, chunck, wock, like the regular 'tocking' of a grandfather's clock.

After a brief inspection of the site, making a mental note of the highest (in case of rain), flattest, and relatively root free spot for the tent, availability of wood (lots of it); I dig out the thermos of ice tea from under the sleeping bag.

Normally I would not have put ice in the thermos, but this is a wide mouth plastic container and I didn't expect it to stay cold on such a warm day, so I filled it with ice. It is a pleasure to be able to enjoy a slow long cold thirst quenching drink on a dazzling day. I expect to be roughing it and that means no ice cold water for a while.

What would the early Native Americans think of my "camping"? Their predecessors, the Lamoken Culture, lived here before Noah's time. They were nomadic hunters and gatherers. They didn't have bows and arrows, and acorns were their staple food. Later came the Woodland Culture. They inhabited this area until one thousand A.D. when the Iroquois Culture evolved. Their great League of Nations was organized long before the thought of living in peace and joining forces occurred to people in Europe. Those Native Americans that did not accept membership into the League or Confederacy were attacked and destroyed. Their system of government was so balanced that it was copied by our founding fathers.

When the trappers moved west in search of more beaver, traders followed to trade for the beaver furs to send to Europe. The settling of North America was due in part to Europe's stylish demand for top hats made from a rodent with a flat tail. As trading trails opened up the land, pioneers began moving in on the Natives' land and claiming it for their own. Naturally they were attacked by the Natives whose land they were invading. The whites were determined to settle the rich land. They cleared the forests hunted the remaining animals and attempted to either "civilize" or destroy the Native Americans.

When the Natives fought back, the Great White Father, George Washington, assigned General Sullivan to rid the territory of the "redskins" by whatever means available. So peaceful Native American villages were attacked, women, children and old people were killed, houses and crops burned, orchards cut and stored food destroyed.

The Native Americans were driven north and west by the Sullivan Expeditions to move them out of the area and toward land occupied by the British, hoping they would cause trouble for the British who were also claiming the land as theirs.

No wonder the feeling of Native American spirits in these woods make our spine tingle. It should.

***

The sun light begins to dim and more birds start to sing. An itch on my leg, then another on my arm, my neck, then foot, mosquitos! Time to find the repellant and set up camp.

Although I put a mattress on the floor of the van, just in case, my intention is to backpack part of THE Appalachian Trail. Actually this is just a spur of the Finger Lakes Trail which intersects the Appalachian but I stretch it to be part of THE great adventurous trail.

It doesn't take long to put up the green nylon rip stop four man tent. Four man means it will hold two people and some

gear or four small children side by side without gear. Instead of the plastic tent pegs, I should have brought the long spikes (nails) we use for pegs because the ground is hard and dry and the plastic stakes bend instead of going in.

Now I can undo the ropes and poles and turn the tent around so the door is facing front. A green fly is put up over the tent to act as a double shade and to keep out a hard rain.

Fortunately close inspection of the ground while bending the pegs does not turn up any of the dreaded three leafed poison ivy. Murphy has a way of seeing that poison ivy is always instantly prolific in the best places to pitch a tent, especially in the dark, or in the rain. While setting up the tent, I am making slapping sounds similar to the breaking of small twigs as the mosquito detail is out in full force.

Now that the pack is visible in the back of the van I can find, er, look for the mosquito repellant. Better than repellant is changing into jeans and a long sleeve shirt. Only after liberally spraying repellant on the brim of a crushable hat, which makes an invisible screen of repellant fumes around my head, do the mosquitos call a truce and keep their distance, about two and one half inches.

There is no mosquito-free home for me to escape into here. The little blighters buzzing in my ears and the itching from the minute amounts of anticoagulant injected to keep their meal flowing are not something I can endure for long, at least they won't go in my ears now. Fortunately the repellant on the hat works well for quite awhile but to be sure to have the right combination, I dab a little of another kind of repellant on my neck forehead and chin. My hat lends character to my unfashionable but comfortable outfit.

I wear a button-at-the-neck, tan plaid long sleeve large cotton shirt. It won't show dirt easily, keeps out bugs and sun and can be opened to let out heat or closed to keep it in. Bathing suit, undershirt or nothing can be worn underneath according to the weather. Made from soft material the shirt has long tails that can be tucked in for warmth or flapped vigorously to cool or tied around the midriff. The small breast pocket is only good for small maps, not chocolate or hard candies.

The stretch jeans have large pockets which are a necessity. My hiking boots, bought at a sidewalk sale, have cleated soles and lace above the ankles for support. They are men's boots because they are usually cheaper than woman's fashion models and run wider in comparison. Generally a woman's size is two numbers less than the men's. For any long distance walking, three pairs of socks work best.

Next to your feet, wear one lightweight, nylon, silk or propalyne socks. Who can afford silk?, but then how can a hiker afford to have blisters. You don't want moisture to collect and even moderate walking will cause your feet to perspire.

Next, wear two pair of wool socks. A much admired and experienced two-time hiker of the whole Appalachian Trail told us, the socks rub against one another and not your feet. They also cushion them, in fact I wear two pair of socks all the time with street loafers when doing a lot of walking.

It's time to reconnoiter the trail a little to see which direction I will take tomorrow. Finally I can take part in making a little bit of my history by hiking on THE trail. The Finger Lakes Trail is part of the North Country National Scenic Trial which goes three thousand miles across the United States. The Finger Lakes Trail was Wally Woods' idea and the first meeting to set it up was held at Keuka College on Keuka Lake in 1961. The FLT covers 556 miles and is nearly complete.

One recent hiker of the FLT, Joe Dabes, who has backpacked in the Sierras, Big Horn, Adirondacks and the Catskills said, "But insects often and crowds always abounded. I was increasingly anxious for the solitude of the FLT."

I've been a little envious of the interesting people that have hiked THE trail, now it's going to be my turn.

To get on the path from Blueberry Hill you have to walk down the road a little way, turn into a shallow ditch and climb a short bank. Along the road are No Parking-Tow-away signs taped to short sticks. Why would they have them here, in the middle of nowhere? The path is narrow and bushes crowd the winding well worn trail. The path is almost overrun by thick bushes that are a little over head high. It is impossible to see more than a few feet ahead and there are few trail markers. I guess I won't get far tonight because I forgot to put a flashlight in my pocket.

Intent on finding my way on the winding trail and over the hardened mud ridges left by horses that traveled the trail when it was muddy, I don't pay any attention to the bushes themselves. Then on an over-hanging branch in front of my face, blueberries, blueberries everywhere! What a find! Then slowly it dawns, the campsite name, the no parking signs along the road, sure...there must be lots of people who come to pick the "delushious" berries.

Now I am all alone in this lush patch of nature's bounty, er, at least I hope so. Distant rustling indicates company in the green and purple patch. Bears common up to the 1800's are rarely seen but not unknown (one was treed a while ago in Penn Yan about 20 miles "as the crow flies" to the west) and this would be a bear's heaven. It's impossible to see beyond the next bush. I think it would be good idea if I rustled the branches and made a little noise, or whistled, so the bear, or whatever, knows that it has company, just to be on the safe side.

Of course I know there're no bears here. I hope.

With nothing to put the berries in for later, I'll just have to eat as I go. What a delightful way to spoil an appetite for dinner! Too soon the bushes thin out and the trail becomes a woodland path and the trail markers are easier to see. It looks like some of the tree trunks are blackened. Controlled burning, learned from the Native Americans, is used to improve the blueberry harvest.

The rough trail forks and I take the one that seems to go down into a gully. It will be dark soon so I won't get to see the stream or the end of the gully tonight. Had I continued south on the Interlochen Trail, I would have reached the main part of the FLT in about three miles.

It's almost dark by the time I get back to camp. I wish I had retrieved some wood for the fire before the excursion. Hummocks of soil, downed trees and young growth make it difficult to find dead branches for the fire in the near dark.

A hand full of dead pine twigs broken off close to the bottom of a nearby tree makes starting the fire easy. None of the other branches I stumble on are much larger than what can be broken by stomping on them. An "Indian" fire, just adequate, in the charcoal fireplace is all I need to make dinner. Smoke is an added bonus to help keep away the ever present mosquitos. I wonder where they are coming from, there's no water around here and it hasn't rained in well over a week.

The single candle lantern sits on the picnic table next to the mess kit. It's surprising how much light it gives off. The backpacker's lantern has an aluminium reflective back with eisenglass windows. The only problem is that the tent-like cover doesn't always stay closed when carrying it by the handle. Once it is lit, the wind doesn't seem to bother it. Tonight it gives off a golden warm light, that attracts all kinds of flying bugs that crash into the glass and then spin crazily on their backs on the table.

The person chopping wood is still at it. They must be preparing for a cold night, a large bonfire, or have lots of frustration to get rid of. Chopping wood is one of the few constructive ways of venting steam and still providing a stack of additional energy.

It seems that everything I need for dinner is in the van buried under something. Tomorrow I have to get organized. The cooler is wrapped in an old sleeping bag which makes the ice last longer. I have lined the cooler with layers of newspapers to increase the insulating power.

In order not to have trouble with the van battery, I remove the light bulb in the back of the van because the obstinate switch won't stay in the off position.

The planned menu is an instant dinner, just add water and mix, but after finding the leftover hamburger in the cooler... it wouldn't do to let it spoil. Dinner turns out to be stir fried hamburger in the mess kit fry pan, with leftover pieces of pepper, a couple of old tomato slices, mixed with dried minced onion, a dash of Italian seasonings, a shake of garlic powder, a little salt and two small packets of ketchup left over from an outing to a fast food eatery. It makes more than enough after eating so many blueberries. Eating this way will definitely not help my envisioned slimming program.

After having a cup of hot tea, a cup of hot water poured into the pan with a drop of detergent is enough to wash the fork and, with the help of a plastic scrubbing pad, clean the pan. One more cup of tea and the rest of the boiling water rinses out the pan. The section of paper towel wipes face, hands, then fuels the fire making a flare of light.

The nearness of the Seneca Army Depot is forgotten until a helicopter with long blades whacking the air with deafening whallops, skims over the trees doing sentry duty. It is ironic that here in the essence of being outside, the means of world destruction is less than twenty-five miles away. I wonder how the Woman's Peace Encampment is doing? It's not far from here, near the Depot. The women are protesting the nuclear missiles stored there and being shipped overseas.

Now the people of the world can, if not censored, see on television the concern and frustration of many women toward the armament race. But I'll bet none were shown the peace and beauty of this area.

On the edge of the Depot at night you can see the red dotted blinking 700 foot sentinel LORAN tower piercing the sky. It emits a radio wave that helps the captains on the oceans and Great Lakes navigate. They can locate their positions, targets, oil spills or undersea minerals within a quarter of a mile.

As the quiet returns it becomes a soothing warm peaceful night, with the usual chorus of crickets, peepers and mosquitos and time to hit the sack. The new ensolite pad looks thin, but everyone says a firm mattress is good for your back. Because it is too warm to get into the sleeping bag, all I take off is my shoes so the mosquitos won't have quite so much to feast on.

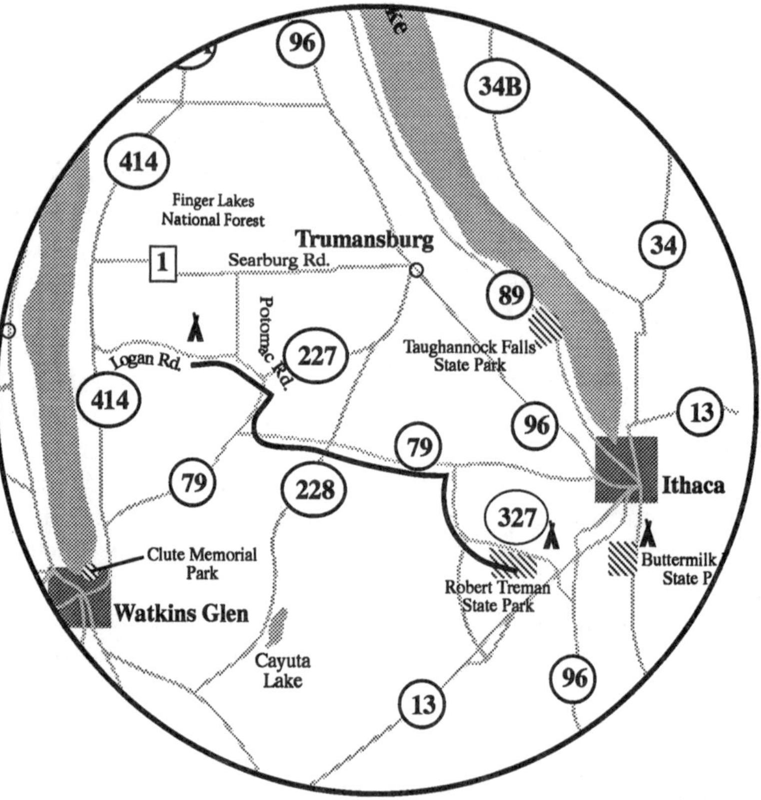

Change of Plans

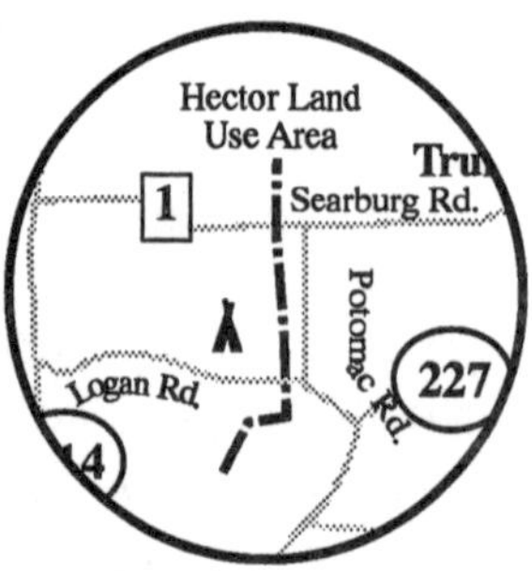

Interloken Trail

CHANGE OF PLANS & POUNDING WATER

The earth is the Lord's and all that is in it,
the world and those who dwell therein.
For it was he who founded it upon the seas
and planted it firm upon the waters beneath.
Psalm 24 vs 1-2

Two o'clock in the dark rustling night finds me wrestling with the ensolite pad. Even doubling it over is still not enough padding for my hips and shoulders. Laying on your back is perfect for star gazing but not for sleep. So after fumbling with my shoes, I clomp over to the van dragging the sleeping bag, stumble into the van and snuggle into the mattress. Oh why did I leave the much heavier thick foam pad at home? I counted weight against comfort this trip and lost.

An essential part of my camping gear is my almost all-in-one tool, a Swiss Army pocket knife. Most pocket knives fold into a thin wafer- like rectangle and fit nice and flat into a pocket. My all in one super deluxe special knife is three and one-half inches long, nearly one inch wide and over one inch thick. It has a heavy two foot long nylon cord tied at one end, so it can be worn around the neck, looped through a belt loop or used to make emergency repairs like tying up a tent.

The knife has a total of thirteen assorted tools, a toothpick and a long lost tweezer. The toothpick and tweezer fit into the outside of the case. There are two blades, scissors, file, magnifying glass, saw, screwdriver, corkscrew, awl, bottle

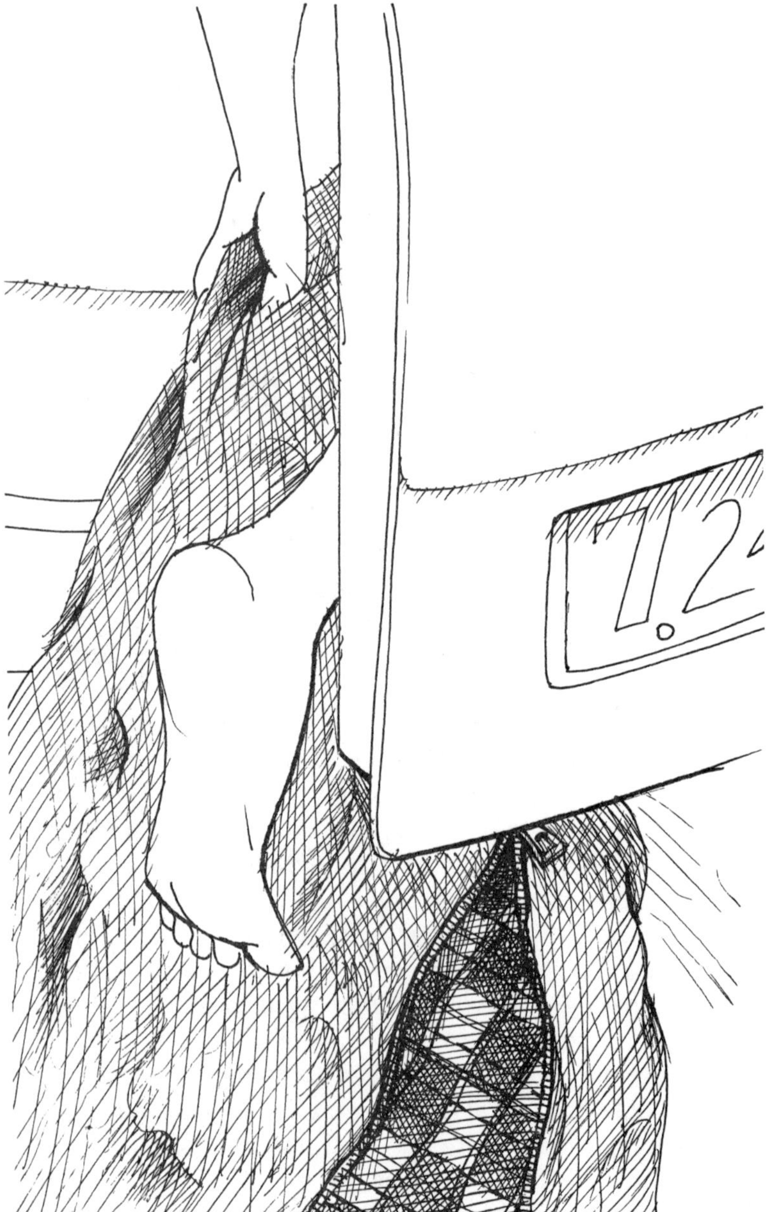
7.2

opener and phillips screw driver. This essential camping buddy is kept in my pocket to insure its availability in time of need. The knife's large bulge has worn a white slash on my front dungaree pocket.

Having had numerous occasions of needing one of the tools immediately, while holding parts of the object to be repaired or whatever in my lap, and usually finding the knife to be out of reach, I made the camp rule that it was to be kept in my pocket at all times. Having diligently adhered to the rule I had inadvertently formed a corresponding dent in my hip to match the knife as I slept on it.

As I crawled out of the van in the early morning, I suffered severe and sudden pain in my hip when I stepped on my right leg. First thought was I pulled a muscle while walking over the rutted trail yesterday. Too bad friend Murphy isn't here to consult. I tell myself it will go away after walking on it for awhile, after all, I wasn't on the ensolite pad THAT long.

I feel very conspicuous as I hobble slowly to the outhouse, water faucet and back to camp. To add insult to injury when I wipe my face with a cold wet washcloth, I manage to get some of last night's repellant into my eyes. It stings for only a little while. Make note - wipe eyes first then the rest of the face. After chasing imaginary critters around with my hair brush, the next thing to tackle is the fire for breakfast.

The promise of a new day doesn't seem as bright now that walking is so painful. Sleeping out in the tent on the trail will be impossible until I have a softer sleeping pad. A good night's sleep is imperative to backpacking if it is to be enjoyable.

It's discouraging to scratch the plans for backpacking for now, but it doesn't need to interfere with hiking. I'll just camp and return to the van or tent for the night.

The pine tree with the kindling-wood-twigs seems to have moved further away during the night. It seems more trips are needed for a few sticks to boil water for the anticipated first cup of coffee and breakfast now that it is difficult to walk.

Breakfast is picturesque as well as filling. The yellow sheet of paper toweling is flanked by the brown plastic silverware pouch. The bright orange mug is ready with instant coffee and cream colored dry milk granules for the boiling water. All is surrounded by the dark brown stained, deeply engraved uneven picnic table. A red and golden nectarine is next to the shiny aluminium mess kit on the yellow towel. Two plastic bags labeled "breakfast" and "spices" are sprawled at the head of the towel. Streaks of sunbeams dance over the table. The breeze moves the leaves in an early morning summer dance dropping assorted decorations from the trees above.

The pine twigs finally start the dew damp wood and the smoke gently curls into the trees. The instant oatmeal looks more like wet cement than oatmeal, but after adding raisins, dried apples, dried milk and a squeeze of honey, it looks better. Strange how filling it is.

After trying to toast a stale English muffin on the fork and singeing my hand, I find a stick and attach an extension to the fork with the handy dandy black plastic repair tape. Now to put a little peanut butter and jelly on it. The "real" peanut butter is thick and doesn't come out of the food tube until squeezed with both hands and then a big gob shoots out with a pop. It's a good thing I like peanut butter because there is no way to get it back in the tube without making more of a mess. Conditioned to squeeze hard, a large red glob of strawberry jelly comes out with a swish. The second cup of coffee is almost too much food for breakfast.

I am determined to hike, so I pack a lunch, clean up and study the available maps. This is a case where being prepared with a detailed map would be nice. I pick the northern part of the Interloken Trail because it is listed as a spur of the FLT and perhaps it will be a little smoother than the southern trail; adventure and new vistas being more important right now than the Blueberry patch.

It looks like it will be a sunny hot day again so I'll hike until noon, then turn around and come back. (If I had a detailed map I could have made a small loop instead of staying on the same trail.) No reason to stay here if I can't camp out on the trail, so later today I'll move to a state park. Maybe I'll be able to get a thicker pad somewhere.

With first day enthusiasm and excitement of having gotten this far on the Retreat, I am hobbling on my way by nine thirty. The north part of the Interloken Trail is much wider than the entrance to the south section and it seems to be used by many more horses. There must be a solid rock subsoil here because there are many muddy places even though we haven't had rain for days. It would be very difficult to hike this after a heavy rain. No wonder there are so many mosquitos!

Mosquito larva hatch from eggs laid on the surface of any standing water, ponds or even in tree holes. The mosquitos have even adapted to civilization by using the ever present stagnant water in discarded junk tires. The mosquito larva eat plant materials in the water but must breathe air at the surface. This is the time they spray because the larva can be suffocated by a thin film of oil.

When they mature and leave the water, it is only the female that bites because she needs the blood to feed the next generation she is making. Fortunately mosquitos are food for insects, fish, frogs, birds and bats or we would be over run with them.

Mosquitoes are carriers of diseases. Each particular kind of mosquito carries a particular disease. In recent years there have been a couple of cases of equinine (horse) encephalitis near Syracuse and an extensive spraying program was resumed. Now a hardy Asian mosquito, the Tiger Mosquito has migrated to the United States bringing with it other diseases.

Thousands of workers on the historic Erie Canal contracted malaria while digging thru the swamps of Montezuma in Seneca County. It stopped the construction of the canal until they figured out what caused the debilitating disease. They waited until the mosquito season was over and inspite of the difficulties of digging thru a swamp they were able to finish that section of the Canal on time.

Another insect, the tick, whose area of infestation rarely reaches this part of the Central Finger Lakes, can carry the recently named Lyme Disease. Although the symptoms have been around for a long time, no one had made the connection to a tick bite that produces a round red rash, fever and chills to severe arthritis years later. Now when the symptoms appear shortly after a bite, if diagnosed and treated with antibiotics the aches and pains can be avoided.

Hiking the uneven ground with heavy shoes and a sore hip is tiring. In many places the ridges left by the horses hooves squishing into the mud are covered with growing grass and it is easier to try to walk along the outside edges of the path in the brush than where the horses have gone.

The trail switches from forest to shrubbery to over grown field. I haven't met anyone or crossed any other trails. Quite unexpectedly I come upon Foster Pond and scare two small ducks into the air and beyond the trees before I can pick out any identifying marks. Foster Pond is one of twenty-seven wildlife ponds in the park. It is a small pond formed by bulldozing a long dike on the side of a gentle slope. The southwesterly breeze on my back is cooling as I rest on the dike and become acquainted with the pond.

On the dike side, the soil has been disturbed and the dike is made from the poor heavy clay subsoil, so the thinly spaced plants are not well nourished. Wild bachelor buttons and Queen Anne's Lace, also called Wild Carrot, nod in the breeze over sparsely growing clover. None of the three are native plants here. Queen Anne's Lace is also known as bird's nest plant because when it dries after blooming it forms a small cup that resembles a small bird's nest. Native Americans used the dried seeds, which have an anise-like flavor, as a spice.

A handy tool of the hikes and walks is a small hand lens. After picking a Queen Anne's Lace I search for the "bug in the center". There it is, the mistaken bug is actually a velvety purple four petal flower. The lens I use doesn't cost much and makes a perfect gift for young and old to discover a new miniature world outdoors. You don't even have to go beyond your back yard to go to the monster zoo or beautiful garden.

Take a piece of paper, or a tray, or plastic bag, pick a stem of one of the blooming goldenrods and shake it over the paper. An assortment of bugs will come tumbling out.

Clover blossoms, trefoil, daisies, dandelions, plantain flowers, teasels and even maple tree flowers compare in color and beauty to garden flowers when looked at under a lens.

The up-hill sides of the pond have plants growing right into the water. There are cattails and lilies on the far side making a green peninsula into the water, and frogs are brreeping challenges back and forth across the lily pads. It's tempting to go for a swim, but the bottom looks like clay-mud and I'd probably be dirtier afterwards. It is a hassle to get the boots and socks to fit just right as I haven't gotten back into the practice of it. Even with three pairs of socks on, one heel feels like it might be bunching up. Splashing the cool water on my face, dampening shirt and dungarees combined with the breeze works nicely to cool off.

The square sunken cement overflow at the edge of the pond allows the little wavelets to travel over the walls and out the overflow pipe. Little minnows dart into the shallow seaweed as my shadow passes over them. I wonder if there are larger fish in the depths.

Briefly I wish I had brought my fishing rod with me, but if I did catch any, I'd have to clean them, unless, I cooked them "Indian style". Indian style is putting the fish in the fire, letting it cook, then peeling away the outside and eating the meat. It works best if the outside is charred, because it comes off easier. The meat is juicer Indian style, without having to add oil or use a pan. Or, of course, I could let them go again.

The breeze is keeping most of the bugs away and it's cooling as the water evaporates the water,. Hmm, a nap would be nice. The sun is too hot and the breeze doesn't bother the bugs whose world is the first three inches of grass above the baked ground. Besides it is too early in the day to take a nap.

This is a fine spot to meditate about the variety of life all around and its existence both beyond my little sphere as well as microscopically within it.

The trail beckons to new views on the other side of the pond where a cluster of large willow trees are growing out of lush deep green long bladed grass. Horses tethered over a period of

time account for the luxuriant grotto. The willows make a nice shelter and it is easy to visualize songs being sung around glowing embers to the accompaniment of a guitar. But now it's just ashes and litter. A nice place to camp some time, especially if there are fish in the pond or promise of a full moon.

Past the willows the Backbone Trail joins the Interloken Trail. Much of the Finger Lakes National Forest is land that the government reclaimed years ago when farmers were unable to grow crops on the marginal soil and went bankrupt. Some of it was reforested by the Civilian Conservation Corps in the 1930's, some was let for grazing and some land was allowed to go wild. In the middle of October they have an old fashioned round-up of the free roaming grazing cattle from large fenced pastures.

In the field of shrubs where farm fields have been left to revert through succession, old hedgerows are darker green strips of tall growth while the fields have short and sparce growth because of less nutrients and air in the compact clay soil. This seems to be the high spot of the whole area. The Backbone Trail crosses the Interloken Trail and goes down over the hill towards Seneca Lake on what looks like the remains of an old farm lane.

Pink clover grows along the edges of the road and goldenrod grows more thickly in the overgrown fields. A member of the daisy family, one or more of the 60 goldenrod varieties bloom one after the other which gives the appearance of a continuous golden glow from July through October. The people who claim to be allergic to goldenrod pollen are probably chemically allergic to it because, unlike the rag weed pollen that has prickly points that scratch and irritate, goldenrod pollen is smooth and round.

Mixed with the Queen Anne's Lace is Chicory. It grows scattered along the edges of the path where it can get the sun at ground level. At first it is dandilion-like, then it grows an irregular long stem with daisy-like blue flowers, sometimes white, that close at noon.

Chicory and the familiar ox-eye daisy are alien flowers too.

Chicory was first cultivated by monks in Holland in the 9th Century and brought from Europe because they found its roots, when dried, roasted and ground made their coffee richer tasting or could even be used in place of coffee. When young, chicory greens are good in salads and are high in important minerals and Vitamin A.

Even the desirable red clover along the edges is an alien plant, making wonder what these fields would look like if there were only native plants growing here. Oh, for a ladder to see the whole view down to Seneca Lake! Far off in the distance to the west are hazy quilt-like shades of green, patching the far side of the hills that hold Seneca in the deep valley.

About 450 million years ago when there was a tropical sea covering the land, the Euryperids, now the official New York State fossil, was exploring the bottom. A distant relative to the lobster and horseshoe crabs of today, the four to eight inch long scorpion-like and far distant relative of spiders, had compound eyes and a stinger like tail. At the same time the Euryperid was crawling on the bottom of the tropic sea the salt deposits were being laid down. Later there were great land upheavels and the continents continued to drift further apart.

During the two times that the great ice sheet covered the land it blocked the natural water flow. The water in Seneca Lake rose to about 900 feet above sea level before it overflowed. Cayuga presently at an average of 385 feet above sea level collected enough water to be 1,040 feet above sea level!

The ice sheet covered the Finger Lakes for at least 9,000 years and when the climate warmed it melted back at the rate of 200 feet a year. As it receded north, it blocked southern drainage with debris which left most of the Finger Lakes with north flowing outlets.

It's theorized that only a few degrees less than the temperatures we have now, plus lots of snow, would produce another ice sheet.

Seneca is over 635 feet deep in the deepest part. Its surface is kept at an average of 445 feet above sea level by gates on the Seneca River. The water is far lower than the highest hill here which is 1,400 feet high. Scientists (Limnologists) have found the original bottom of the lake is still another 600 feet deeper but it is now filled in with silt. Even with the silt the deepest part of the lake is two-hundred feet below sea level!

No wonder there are all kinds of fantastic rumors about caves linking the Finger Lakes. (If there were caves the levels of the linked lakes would be the same height, and they are not.) There are also rumors of prehistoric sea monsters living in the depths of Seneca and Cayuga, which to this date no one has proven. Seneca Lake and Loch Ness in Scotland have similar internal waves that causes bottom erosion. Exactly what causes the waves is part of an on-going study by the H.W.S. Explorer, a research boat of Hobart and William Smith Colleges in Geneva at the north end of Seneca Lake.

The tales of not giving up the dead have some truth because the water down deep is always cold so decomposition doesn't occur and the gases that would cause the bodies to float to the surface are not formed.

Not only are Seneca's deepest parts at a constant temperature of 39 degrees, but there are salty ponds on the bottom. The salt ponds stay on the bottom because salt water is heavier than fresh water.

There is a legend that says Native American drums can be heard calling for a lost brave. They can be heard on calm days and quite often before a storm. It is said they are only bubbles of natural gas released from pockets when the pressure builds up enough. To this day there is a sacred Native American place of the eternal spirit on the west side of the lake, where a match will light the gas seeping from the ground.

The Interloken Trail continues north and then curves and enters the cool woods again. This part of the trail has had a lot of traffic. The earth is worn away from between the roots and muddy spots on the trail have grown into large circles where people and horses have gone around to avoid the mud. This use is what is destroying some of the more delicate areas in the Adirondack Mountains. At what point do you balance use with the protection of the environment?

Much attention must be given to placing the feet so you don't trip. It is slow progress to watch where you step and look around as you go. I have the trail to myself but the constant picking up and over and around the roots, uneven ground and mud holes is wearisome, especially since my hip still hurts. I have more sympathy for the hardships the pioneers had while traveling west on rough trails.

I find a fallen log and sit on it to rest and the mosquitos immediately attack. Knowing I have to return the way I have come, I declare lunch and will take my time returning to camp. It is disappointing not to have reached the next cross road but according to the general map it shouldn't be far away. Right now it looks like I won't be able to backpack. I'll try for camping where I can swim and take day hikes in state parks until I find another sleeping mat.

The refreshing can of lemon soda is gone and most of the water from the pint plastic flask which I could easily finish but I'll save the rest of the water for the half-way mark back. The lunch sandwich made from an English muffin, carbohydrates for energy, margarine- fat for longer lasting energy - cheese for protein, calcium and fat- and pepperoni, for taste, is filling. Snappy flavors seem to be more enjoyable when camping, especially when most food is backpack style.

Dessert, a package of fruit leather is eaten on the way in an effort to get away from mosquitos. I am somewhat of a nutrition, anti-additive person and have dried fruits and home grown vegetables in order to provide my growing family with good food without sugar and additives. It saves money, space and time. It is easier to prepare food for drying than other ways of keeping it; that is if I can keep my family from eating the fruit before I can get it out of the dryer and into the freezer for winter lunches and snacks.

Walking back on the same trail has advantages. It is one way to get to know the trail. Because you don't need to concentrate on the trail you can pay more attention to other things along the way. Sniffing the air for the different smells of the woods and damp places or plants in bloom is not one of the senses you use on a new trail. Generally you are more comfortable, less tense and more leisurely when you are walking back over an area you've been on before. It is surprising how different the trail looks going the other way. There is much to see, hear and smell. Right now, it seems to be more real and valuable than the trivia and plastic we surround ourselves with at "home". That "home", we voluntarily work long hours to provide, seems more like a cage at times. Where does man belong? Making "progress" in their own created world of business, or here?

Yet I would be hard put to survive here in the middle of our snowy cold winter. But if I had a thick hollow hair coat of a deer and I could eat buds and twigs, then winter might be mine too. Winter's beauty could be temporarily enjoyed shushing cross country on skis or snow shoes.

I wish I had remembered my note pad to keep a list of the wildlife encountered. Next time, remember fishing line, a container for berries and a larger water container. Somewhere along the line a decision must be made as to whether you are hiking or foraging because existing on forage is a time consuming and unreliable method of covering miles. The bottom of my pant legs are muddy but the coarse grass has worn off most of the mud from the boots. I consider myself lucky that it hasn't rained recently or I would never have gotten this far. Other parts of the FLT are not nearly so worn or uneven.

* * *

The teeth-cracking cold water from the hand pump back at the camp's well is refreshing, and is worth all the effort of pumping it. Not nearly so much water would be wasted if everyone had to work this hard for it. Thousands of gallons are allowed to drip away or have to be treated and then pumped back into the rivers for the next town to draw, use and return usually dirtier than before.

In some places in the former Soviet Union, used water has to be put back in the river upstream of the city that used it.

People would think twice about fouling their own drinking water if we had to do that here. Working for the water made it taste that much better, and there is no chlorine taste to it.

Another treat is observing the campsite with my hiking boots off and my feet propped up on the picnic bench while leaning back in the lawn chair.

An aluminium lawn chair would not be carried while backpacking but it is a necessity when park camping because the benches get hard fast and do not have any back support.

The wood chopper is still at it. I wonder if they are preparing for winter. Some parks allow people to cut wood for fuel, but I don't know how that program works. Perhaps the fellow cutting is in training for the Woodsmen's Competitions held every year in Trumansburg and in Boonville. They compete in sawing, log rolling, pole climbing and other skills involved in lumbering.

There must be some way I can get a better pad to sleep on. It isn't likely that just any store would carry a thick one or even another one to add to the one I have, and I don't particularly want to go to a shopping plaza.

The tent is dry and folds nicely, but refuses to stuff the bag. The bag is not made to hold the ground cloth and that's as much of a necessity as the poles. Packing up or breaking camp is not nearly as involved as getting ready to leave home.

The only activity has been a park maintenance truck slowly circling on the gravel campground road and the sound of some children playing on the far side of the circle and the wood chopper.

After studying the New York State Finger Lakes Bicycle Touring Map put out by the Office of Parks and Recreation and Historic Preservation, I pick out Robert Treman State Park as the next destination. I acquired the map as part of a group of people that bicycled some of the Finger Lakes roads and helped to classify them according to ease, traffic and safety. Another good map of the Finger Lakes is the Finger Lakes of New York State Road and Street map by Visual Encyclopedia, distributed by Marshall Penn-York Co. Inc. of Syracuse, NY.

The Finger Lakes Trail maps come on separate sheets of paper for a particular section of Trail. They are much more detailed but it takes a little longer to get them mentally orientated on a larger map. There are trail books on some sections, available through the FLTC Service Center, P.O. Box 18048, Rochester, NY 14618 . I'll be able to catch more of the FLT at Robert Treman State Park. Loaded and packed I head east on the dirt road and when I get to the "t", turn right and head south on Potomac Road. The dusty road is crowded by trees and I feel I am in the corner of a small wilderness here. The overhanging green trees seem to be offering protection. It is peaceful and yet exciting because within the forest is the constant struggle of growth and life.

This is a spectacular drive when autumn's blazing colors are at their peak about the second week in October. The colors seem more vibrant here than in the early frost areas, bright reds denoting higher sugar content in the tree. Golden pumpkins, red apples, fresh pressed cider and teepees of corn, delight the palate and the eyes of natives and foliage followers. Now it is difficult to imagine the emergence of the riotous colors from the green walls.

In the fall season you notice and may watch some of the early colored leaves slipping through the air. It is in the first warming hours of the day after a hard frost that most trees relinquish their hold on their leaves and let most of them fall continuously. As the day warms it is almost as if the tree has changed it's mind and holds on to the few remaining leaves a day longer.

Too soon I'm on the black top of Route 227, and turning east on 79. This road looks very... familiar, it should. I was on it yesterday. Eight miles on 79 to Route 327, which then turns south. Just before 327 intersects with 13, 34, and 96 is the turn for the lower camping area of Robert Treman State Park which is also known as Endfield Glen. The Park was established in 1920 when Mr. & Mrs. Treman donated 387 acres to the state.

I picked the lower area for camping because the swimming

area is here. After checking in at the office I have to find a site. To get to the camping area by car it is necessary to forge the stream. A cement drive across the stream bed doesn't require the upkeep a bridge does and the cement will not be damaged when the seasonal heavy rains or ice turns the stream into a raging torrent with all kinds of debris rushing downstream.

I look for a place far from the entrance, but there aren't many vacancies to choose from. Number 53 is open and as a bonus it isn't far from the comfort station. When I report the number to the office I inquire as to where the FLT crosses the park but the student help is unaware that the trail even exists. I find it on the map after I get back to the campsite. Every state park has a map with information and trails marked on it that you get when you sign in.

The camping area is actually off a road that can be used as a fire road or as an alternate entrance to the camping area if the stream is in flood. It intersects the main highway where all the main roads and the stream come together.

I'm glad I have the bike in the valley, because I don't feel like hobbling to the swimming area. A bike is practically a necessity in a State Park because they are usually laid out over a wide area and getting from one place to another can be time consuming. It seems ridiculous to drive anywhere, especially since you are supposedly "camping" or "roughing" it.

The swimming area is on the far side away from my campsite, a half mile or so up into the glen.

The falls are formed as the stream umbrellas over a twenty-foot high rounded shale formation and falls into a pool about forty feet wide and fifteen feet deep. The shale forms shelves and it is possible to sit on a narrow shelf in the pool and let the water cascade onto you. Between the pounding of the water, the noise of it falling and rushing past your ears, the rest of the world disappears, until you can't hold your breath any longer. Try as I might there is no way I can sit under the falls without having to hold my breath, unless perhaps you have a snorkel sticking out of the sheeting water. It is a whole new physical experience to be pounded by the water,which nearly succeeds in washing off my swimming suit.

The swimming area is roughly ninety feet long and is formed by a long wooden and stone dam with four spillways. and is made with the same stone as the stream bed. The height of the water is determined by the number of planks stacked in the dam's slots. They take the planks out for the winter which keeps the pool from freezing and breaking the dam. It also prevents a buildup of branches and stones in the pool from heavy spring rains. Although it feels like there is a considerable amount of water coming down the falls, especially as it beats on you, there is not a large amount going over the small dam.

Now for a small fee anyone can sit under a waterfalls and pretend they are in a far off tropical place. There is something mysterious about sitting under a cascading falls. The water is cool and greenish, a characteristic of Finger Lakes streams. It is a pleasure to listen to the water splashing down the rocks, it has a way of drowning out other thoughts. There is a small grassy place to sun bathe but no real beach, just rocks and grass to sit on. The swimming area is divided by small bouys to mark the safe depths for children, non-swimmers etc.

The shades of the water seem to be ever changing according to the changes of sun, clouds, sky, and wind. The glen doesn't get full sun all day because of the high walls but they don't keep a breeze away.

After drying off, I buy an ice-cream at the concession stand on the way out of the swimming area. Now to explore the camp ground by bike.

* * *

The center lawn is a large mowed field for softball, volleyball, racing, flying kites, soccer, frisbee throwing and can accommodate several games at once. On weekends, if the picnic tables and charcoal burners set along the edge of the field are used, it might seem crowded.

Riding slowly down the fire road I find some blackcap or

black raspberry bushes. The branches or brambles are reddish purple with a kind of chalk dust on them. The berry's short stems are round into the berry and have hooked prickers. They are called black caps because when the berries are ripe they come away from the stem leaving a hollow cap. The larger blackberries stay stuck to the stem when picked.

Many birds eat the berries as well as raccoons, bear, fox, opossum and mice. The brambles are members of the rose family and deer often feed on the leaves and young growth making them an important food source.

I'm surprised that there are so many berries left. It must be that people don't see them or don't know what they are and are afraid to eat them. It's a good rule that if you can't absolutely identify a plant, don't eat it. Needless to say none of the plants should be picked. Some plants, although numerous like dogwood and spring's trillium, are protected as are 33 other native plants. Left, they can be enjoyed by others and perhaps spread. Picked they may be gone from that spot forever. Oh, oh, there is some poison ivy. It seems to thrive anywhere. As I am allergic to it, I have learned to look for it so I can stay away from it. It is the oil, even minute amounts of it, that causes the allergic reaction. If it gets on clothing, shoes or pets you can still get it. A good precaution, if you think you've been in contact with it, is to wash with a strong detergent, both self and clothes, to get rid of the oil.

According to a medical book it takes up to three weeks for the oil to evaporate from clothing, pets and tools. Hence my rule number three hundred-forty-six, forty-seven and forty eight, remember to take off shoes before entering the tent, don't wear outer clothing in the sleeping bag and wash hands frequently, just in case.

There is no better way to ruin an otherwise pleasant vacation than to get poison ivy. If you think you've been in it or start to itch, what works for our family, is to wash well and then dab straight clorox on the area and let it dry, (not around the face though). Apply the clorox every time it starts to itch. I've found over-the-counter hay fever tablets with only antihistamine in it are helpful, because it is a form of allergy attack. If in spite of all the care and washing a spot breaks out it is important to keep it clean and try not to scratch it because you might get a secondary infection on top of the allergy. However, whenever in doubt, see a doctor.

Never, never, never burn poison ivy to get rid of it, because the smoke carries the small particles of oil into the air and anyone breathing it or coming in contact with the smoke may have to be hospitalized if they are allergic to it.

Folk medicine says imediately after you've come in contact with poison ivy, find a jewel weed plant, also known as touch-me-not, with small orange and yellow snapdragon-like flowers, crush the leaves and rub them over where you think you've touched the plant and you will not get it, - as bad. If symptoms have developed, take a large amount of the jewel weed leaves and stems and simmer them in water and use the green liquid on the itchy spots. We have found it to be somewhat soothing, but it lasts for just a short while.

The jewel weed is a member of the touch-me-not family and is called that because when the small pea-like pods of seeds are ripe, the slightest touch will send them shooting out. It grows in moist places and in one seasons can grow up to five feet high. It doesn't have very thick foliage but grows in clumps. The stems are crisp, hollow and moist when broken.

At the far end of the road, where highways, stream and boundaries of the park come together, are the FLT markers. The physical features of this area make this a natural spot for the water and travelways to come together. A closer inspection of the park map shows that the FLT follows the boundary lines of the park and doesn't go down into the glen. This makes the park trail more inviting to me.

Back at the camp, which is a picnic table, and well worn cement fireplace with a grill, it is time to set up camp. Past experience has shown that a grill is not always available on the fireplace, so I carry a homemade one that is just big enough to hold a medium frypan and a coffee pot. The legs fold in on itself for storage or when swung around the other way lock open or go all the way around to make a long grill that lays flat over an existing fireplace, rocks or logs. It is too heavy to backpack but practically a necessity otherwise. There are two wire loops that slide over the legs to close them for storage.

The muddied jeans that I rinsed out this morning are not dry yet but I'll put them on before the expected arrival time of the mosquitos.

It is hot and the air feels heavy. Puffy clouds are forming, perhaps we'll have a thunder storm. There are 600 lightning flashes every second around the world and nearly 16 million thunder storms annually, creating 100 million tons of fixed nitrogen which acts as a fertilizer as it is deposited with the rain and makes everything look so green after a thunder storm.

If caught outside in an electrical storm, stay away from tall trees, don't swim and get to shore if you are in a boat. Stay indoors and keep away from electrical appliances, telephones, showers and dish washing, and unplug TV antennas which should have lightening arrestors on it. Also don't stay in tents that are in the middle of a wet field.

* * *

There are two large tents on the corner lot next to mine, but no one is there right now. On the other side is an assortment of camping gear but no tents, so the occupants must have an RV or some kind of vehicle to sleep in.

A ranger on a moped is patrolling the camp grounds and stops at the water faucet which is the other side of the RV campsite. He takes out a couple of small containers, fills them with water, adds a chemical, shakes them and holds them up to the light. Apparently satisfied with the results, he pours them on the ground and leaves.

A van slowly comes around the circle and pulls into a spot about six sites further up the road. After unloading and making themselves comfortable they put a "boom box" on their picnic table and turn on an opera. It's not loud but not wanting to listen to it, I go searching for wood.

My campsite is about twenty feet wide and twenty-four

feet deep on the level. The back of it is a steep mountain that goes up nearly vertical for at least 300 feet. It is difficult to maneuver in my flat soled water sneakers, plus I don't need to slip in a patch of poison ivy. Most of the reachable wood is gone. I could go down the road where I took the bike ride and look for wood but I feel I would be conspicuous carrying it back and I don't want to advertise that I am alone. Anyone observing me for any length of time could figure it out anyway. Fortunately the people who used this campsite before left a stack of medium sized wood for a fire, so all I have to do is to find some small wood to get it going, right?

Wrong!

The reason they left the wood is because they couldn't burn it. No matter how good the kindling is burning the most it will do is smoke. Even fanning it with a plate will not get it to flame. In fact the only way I can get enough heat to boil the water and cook the hamburger is to fan it with the plate continuously. Another lesson learned, beware of gift wood, and when you are lazy you have to work harder. The hamburger is getting a little slimy and has a strange odor. The smoke took care of the different taste and cooking it into brown crispy granules got rid of the different odor. I ate with my left hand because the right arm wouldn't work very well after fanning the fire. I feel a little guilty cooking food from the cooler, after all this is supposed to be a camping expedition. So I cooked the spinach noodles from one of the dinner packages.

After dumping them into the just steaming water, I remembered that it was enough noodles for two meals. It's a good thing they didn't take long to cook because my arm feels like it is going to fall off.

There isn't much wind, fortunately, so none of the nearby campers are being smoked out, but I'm sure they are wondering what is cooking at the campsite socked in with smoke. Perhaps they think I am performing some sort of ritual, waving the aluminium plate at the fire altar.

Positive that the fire would go out, I put on the damp jeans, long sleeve shirt and hiking boots and set out to walk some of

the FLT. The plan is to walk until dark and then turn around and come back.

The FLT crosses the fire road nearly at the gate, then climbs steeply thru a stand of pines. It is soft underfoot and pleasant to smell, but it is noisy because the traffic is laboring up the hill on the main highway. After awhile the road veers off and it becomes quiet. Walking here is like walking through a brown columned room with a rust colored rug. The only sounds are from birds and muted camp noises drifting up with the smoke, probably mine, from the park below.

When the trail comes to a barricaded road and a sign that points to the YMCA Camp off to the side further up the hill, I decide to follow the narrow steep winding driveway back down to the park because it is getting quite dark in the woods. The road intersects with another path that goes toward the swimming area. The stone path has more than twenty five feet of vertical shale stone wall on one side and the small stream from the falls on the other. The rough wall is damp and cave-like as the last light of day fades.

There are other people on the path too, an older couple, three boys pushing their bikes thru the puddles formed by the water dripping down the rugged wall onto the path, and a young couple holding hands. All are heading for the relaxing splashing of the waterfalls. It's too hot for the long sleeve shirt but the mosquitos are out and it offers some protection.

On the way back I notice the scattered cabins. They are log cabins and stained dark under the tall trees. They are not fancy, but have screens, electricity, bunk beds and a refrigerator. This would be a nice place for a vacation with a minimum of equipment, particularly with small children.

While I am lighting my candle lantern, a young boy rides up to me on a bike and asks where my kids are. "They're at camp."

He shakes his head incredously, "Oh, then you're alone?"

"For the moment," was all I could think of to say.

That clinched it, he gave me a "you're strange" look and rode away quickly. I'm sure anyone with children will soon know that there is a "strange" person on the corner lot.

With much fanning I was able to coax the fire into smoldering again to heat water for a cup of coffee. I savored it because I had worked so hard for what had become a nighty ritual to have a cup and enjoy the oncoming night sounds, shadows and breezes.

It almost got dark but the mercury vapor lights around the comfort station popped on, lighting the road to the point that a flashlight is unnecessary. This would not be a night to use night vision. Once your eyes become accustomed to the darkness it is surprising how much you can actually see at night. There are still no lightning flashes from the thunder storm I know we are going to have.

My little candle looks lost on the table compared to the blazing gas lanterns, florescent lights and chains of colored electrical chinese lanterns at other campsites. Most camps, particularly the one across the road, have gear all over the place. There are about four adults, four children, two toddlers and at least one baby. They have a small plywood trailer, with sides that fold down and a door in the middle of the back to get inside. They have two tents, a net dining tent, two playpens, red, yellow, green, and blue chinese lanterns strung between four trees and at least two clothes lines with towels and bathing suits, two tables, six folding chairs, two loungers, a carriage, walker, bicycles, a station wagon, a little car, and a crackling bonfire.

I tried to put up the tent but couldn't get the pegs into the rock hard ground and shale. Next time I'll bring spikes.

Not being able to set up the tent doesn't disappoint me much, because the idea of having to pack up a wet tent if we have a thunder storm is not appealing.

The only positive thing about my smokey campsite is that the smoke helps to keep the bugs away, but I don't think the neighbors appreciate the repellant effects.

With a cup of barely warm coffee and feet up on the bench and the warm glow from the candle I can observe the night life of the park. You don't see as much when you are on the end of the line and in a smoke cloud, but being on the route to the comfort station makes for some interesting traffic.

There are two kinds of night life, the people that seem to be afraid of the "country" at night and the others that "come alive" when the sun goes down.

The owners of the two large tents next to me just came back in a van with Canadian license plates. They apparently have been sightseeing, because I don't see any packages. They must be on a limited budget because they haven't eaten their dinner yet. There are six people, two teenagers, two young adults and a set of parents. Mother is trying to make dinner but the camp stove will not light, even after considerable pumping by father. Gas camp stoves are finicky, especially at night when everyone is hungry and you can't see. The pitch of their voices rise as they work over the stove, which finally lights after the table service has been searched out with a flashlight, because the lantern won't light either. They couldn't cook with wood because they don't have any. In spite of the fun of camping, I never hear them get to the point of talking loudly.

People camp to get away from the harassment and pressures of daily living and end up trying to make due under trying conditions, by using unfamiliar or make-due equipment and then call it fun, at least some of us do. Shortness of temper is in exact proportion to the number of hours since the last meal and the closer in ages of the children to between 13 and 17, unless one of the members is suffering from sunburn or poison ivy, or would rather be spending the time with friends of similar ages, then multiply by four. If there is a brother or sister that is "immature" that is good for doubling shortness of temper. If camping is straight camping without trying to do a lot of other things, then the routine proceeds at a more leisurely enjoyable pace.

By the end of the day campers have become familiar with everyone elses idosyncrasies and the passing of certain vehicles is associated with a particular family or group. People identify one another with descriptive terminology. For example, the one with the two new bikes, the loud radio, the neat RV, (that's the one that has a portable fireplace), the dirty kids with the water pistols, the people with the cat, the one's with the tent that fell down when they were gone, the children with inner tubes, the honeymooners, etc.

Hmm, wonder what I'm called?

Living close is taken in stride in camp grounds, where people wouldn't put up with it at home. It is perfectly acceptable to say hello to a person you now recognize because you've passed them on a walk around the park, or you' ve met them before on the way to the water faucet. There seems to be an air of comradery holding and uniting the people. It cuts through the social amenities of the "outside" world. Still it is only the children who venture into the undefined territory of another campsite. Adults stay clear of the boundaries of one another, even when passing and talking to the occupant, unless specifically invited into their territory. There is an understood air of trust that keeps sites unmolested. The invisible lines are very much in evidence by the way the camping paraphernalia is set up on a site.

Neighbors don't generally have much interaction unless they are both camping two days or more. It is the "one nighters" that provide the new conversation material for those that have been here longer.

There goes the van with the squeeky wheel making the last run of the day to the island of light. I haven't quite figured out why healthy individuals find it necessary to drive the short distance to the rest room, but perhaps they are unable to get around, I should talk, look how close I am to it.

The last trip of the night is almost a ritual trip. With toothbrush, tooth paste, washcloth, soapdish, towel, if you are going to take a shower, shampoo, comb, brush, soap, etc., you feel your way down the path. With feet clad in zories, plastic sandals with a strap that goes between your toes, that keep slipping off, a flashlight that goes off just as you step on a rock or in a hole, you try to hang onto all these items while the mosquitos get their last meal of the day.

The park noise settles down and the snapping fires that send sparks into the waving leaves are encircled by people contemplating distant ancestors that also sat around the fire and had philosophical thoughts.

At the state park those not huddled around a fire may be in campers playing poker, monopoly or bridge, or talking without benefit of telephone interruptions about how our ancestors sat around fires to keep warm and as means of keeping wild animals and assorted spirits away. Night sounds here consist of slamming of bathroom doors, water flushing, the occasional bark of a dog, aluminium chairs scraping the ground and a few crickets. The clinking of horseshoes has stopped and is replaced by camper doors being slammed shut because they won't stay closed any other way and children pleading to stay up longer or have another marshmallow.

Night sounds backpacking may be a fox yapping, an owl hooting, leaves rustling as little creatures search the ground for food, frogs croaking or distant cars on a country road some where.

Concentrating on the night sounds brings my attention to the heavy panting of an animal. At first it sounds like sandpaper being rubbed but at the realization that it is an animal, fear alerts all muscles and pores in spite of the brain's realistic interpretation, which tends to be exaggerated at night.

* * *

On a camping trip to a more remote area of the state where raccoons make regular bold visits to campsites looking for whatever food they can find or panhandle, it is necessary to throw sticks at them to keep them from walking right up to your table and helping themselves. Merely yelling or pretending to charge at the raccoons who have become accustomed to humans, does not discourage them one bit.

One night, unknown to us, a bear with two cubs was also making the late night rounds of the park's trash cans and picnic coolers. So when the customary rustling began next to our fireplace, I chucked a few stones in the general direction to discourage the raccoons. It worked, the noise continued on to the next campsite where the bears proceeded to tear open a cooler and noisily eat the contents. The campers were in their tent and came out scolding the "raccoons" and instantly made straight to their car when the flashlight lit up the bears' beady eyes.

At that point they alerted the whole park with their screams of fright. I briskly left for the safety of the car. Perhaps the bear didn't stop at our place for dinner because we had already put the food away in the car, but I was glad she didn't, because you don't attempt to converse with a protective mother with cubs. The bears didn't seem to notice the commotion they were making among the campers as they made their rounds until they entered a dining tent and the owner, not being aware of the possible danger, thought it a good time to get a picture of the foraging bears.

Intent on getting a good picture he got pretty close to mother bear and when the flash went off she took to a tree. Had the bear not been surprised it would have left after awhile, but now it was up a tree. When the cubs saw Mom, they followed her lead and went up a tree too. Now it was a standoff. About this time the park ranger entered and tried to get the spectators to leave so the bears would come down. Finally the people left and the bears came down from the trees in the wee hours of the morning.

The following night the bears' return came later, after almost everyone had gotten tired of waiting for them. We had gone to bed in our tent and were just about asleep when the raccoons started to dump the trash cans with loud crashes.

The raccoons could be kept out of the trash by fooling them. They knew that an upside-down trash can with the cover resting next to it meant that no one occupied that site and it would not have any food in it, so all we did was to turn the can upside down over the trash and leave the lid resting against the can and they wouldn't bother it.

When someone at the far end of the park, near the entrance of the trail that went up the aptly named Bear Mountain, began to yell and pound on pots and pans we could tell the bears were back. We had put all our food away in the car and not a peanut or piece of candy was in the tent, I hoped. After awhile things seemed to quiet down and I was almost asleep when I heard a grunting pig like noise, probably raccoons, but what if... Gradually it came closer and closer, and then the tent material rustled like someone was brushing against it. The grunting and sniffing proceeded down along the side of the tent. By now I was rigid with fear and not breathing. Slowly, towards my head, which was just about touching the wall of the tent, came the snuffing, sniffing, grunting and rustling of the tent material. Three feet, two feet, I could hear the click of long sharp toenails on the stones. The grunting is just above my head on the other side of the thin material, I couldn't breathe, or move and didn't dare to, after all one of the bears had entered a tent the night before simply by raking it with its claws and going in. They figured it was after the bacon smell in the material. I didn't want company. I was sure, at least pretty sure, there wasn't a thing to attract a bear in to the tent. A BEAR not two INCHES from my head, and I'm flat on the ground. I thought black bears didn't go after people, but on the other hand I had read stories just before we came camping, where they had attacked people, and here I am with one OVER me. The grunting, sniffing and clicking toenails continued down the tent.

Had my children in the canvas camper followed the rules of no food in the tent? It became quiet except for my pounding heart and short little gasping breaths in between listening for the bears. Some crashing and yelling down the line further along the lake proved that they had left and it was safe to breathe again. I found out later, bears are liable to think just about anything is food, especially if they happen to be a dump bear.

Needless to say it took a while to go back to sleep.

Later on in our stay, after some of the people had enough of the bears and packed up and left, we learned that the bears had become regular visitors to the park and the park ranger was afraid one of the campers would do some--thing foolish, like some are prone to do, so they tried to catch it in a drain pipe trap again and move it away. The bears wouldn't go into the trap.

Obviously mother bear's nightly visits would continue as along as campers left food out and she was teaching her cubs to find food this way. They had trapped her twice before and moved her. The ranger was afraid some one might get hurt so they shot her, trapped the cubs

and let them loose far away where there are few people. If all the campers had followed the rules posted by the park and put all their food away in the cars, the bears wouldn't have bothered the park on a regular basis. Part of the reason the bears visited the park was that the state had passed a law that all the garbage dumps had to be covered daily. This was a catastrophy to the twelve or so bears that had learned to rely on the dump for food. Instead of the easy pickings at the dump, they had to learn to forage on their own. The park was near and the food handy. Later on they discontinued covering the garbage, until the bears hibernated for that year.

Having such a close encounter with wild life was wonderful but I prefer to choose the conditions. Anyway that heavy panting instantly reminded me of the bear incident. After convincing myself that it was only a dog panting, I tried to reminisce about less exciting camping expeditions.

The breeze is high up in the trees and has no way of reaching me so I won't need any covers again tonight, since I am perspiring, for some reason.

Robert Treman State Park must be on the approach for the Ithaca airport, because the airplanes are going over low and on a regular basis.

The candle will be gone soon, so I guess I'll turn in, tomorrow I'll do some real hiking.

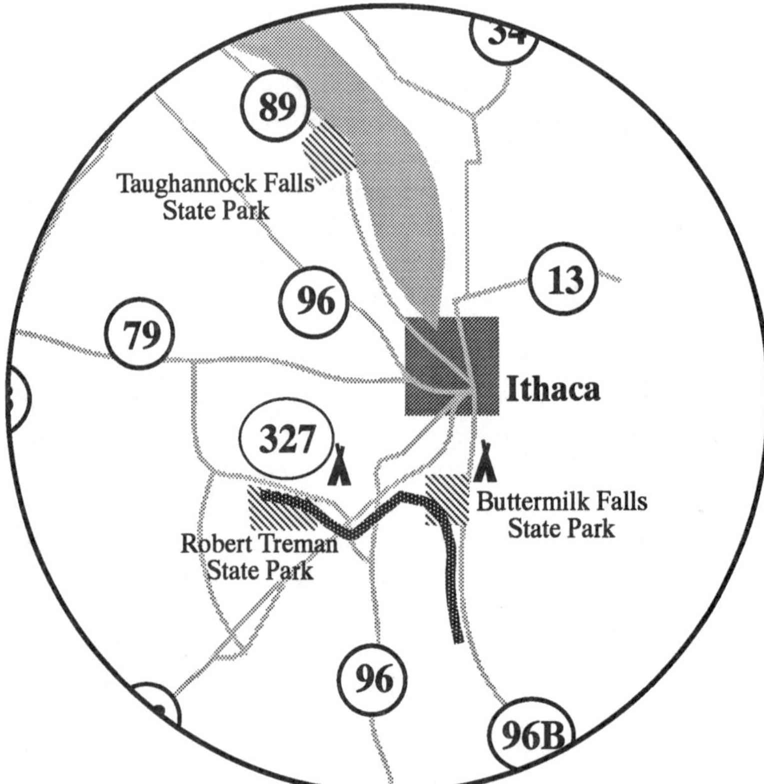

Pine Chapel
& Walking on Glass

PINE CHAPEL
&
WALKING ON GLASS

"He makes me lie down in green pastures,
and leads me beside waters of peace:
He renews life within me.

Psalm 23 vs 2

It is an overcast grey day with light rain, like a thick mist. There isn't enough moisture to wet the ground, just enough to darken it. I'll take my rain jacket, but it is so warm, I doubt if it would be uncomfortable to be wet.

It's important to be prepared for the weather with adequate clothing. Hypothermia can happen in warm weather if there is a cool rain and a breeze, or at least you can become very uncomfortable. It is best to carry or wear extra clothing and take it off than to wish you had it.

The breakfast fire smoked so badly I almost got out the gas stove. Mixed with the fog, the smoke made the air heavy and thick. All I had to do was boil water for cereal and coffee. For lunch I rescued an over-ripe banana from the left-over box and made another cheese and pepperoni sandwich on a muffin and packed a candy bar, nectarine and water in the knapsack along with a pencil and camera.

After consulting the park map, I picked the gorge trail and was on my way before many other people were up. According to the map, it is about six miles round trip through the elongated 1025 acre glen park. The gorge trail begins on the same side as the park office that is backed up against a steep hill. That makes the camping and recreation part of the park in a narrow valley.

The trail starts out very steep with zigzagging stairs all the way to the rim of the gorge. The stairs are made with highway post-markers with holes drilled in either end and pegged in the ground to keep them from sliding down the hill. Most of the stairs are blacktopped between the posts.

The trail, almost a sidewalk, snakes up the hill diagonally and weaves along the gorge wall; first down, then up, aiming for the most conveniently flat places on the very edge of the almost vertical cliff. The sides of the gorge are VERY steep and it's not easy for me to overcome my fear of height. My hands are clammy and my muscles taut as I will my body as far from the edge as possible. Near panic strikes, what if I meet someone and have to walk near the edge? Mentally I know I can not fall. Emotionally I am not convinced.

I can feel an unknown force trying to tip me off the path. Yet it is amply wide and in many places has hand rails (they do not reassure me I am not being tipped). Phobia's are an unreasoning fear, and that's what I have as I walk along. Perhaps if I walked it everyday for a while I would be able to walk in the middle of the path instead of the edge of the uphill side. What a waste of enjoyment of view and trail. I have no problems with airplanes, but ladders, stairs and cliffs are my downfall.

I feel like sitting on the up side ground along the trail and sliding along on my bottom, holding on to whatever is available, but I don't; I stay on the inside edge of the path and sweat.

Where it is a shear drop-off right next to the path a wire fence has been put up. I check it all, the whole length, to see that it has been repaired and strengthened where necessary.

In spite of my unreasoning fear, it is a delightful walk. There are tall pine trees clinging to the side of the hill but in many places they have been blown over and cut to open the trail. Earlier this year a strong wind storm came through this area and many of the old large trees were broken like matchsticks and all of them lay pointed in the same direction. It must have been quite a storm. I'm glad I wasn't out in it.

In places, there is such a thick stand of evergreens they make the trail dark, quiet, still and protected by deep shadows. It is impossible to see the sky through them. The glen is a world by itself. I marvel at the cathedral-like atmosphere as I walk the still, cool path. The pine scent is very strong where there is a freshly cut fallen tree. It is a clean penetrating, invigorating smell that is impossible to tire of. I wish I could capture some of it in a bottle and bring it back home with me. (Commercial cleaners come nowhere near the true pine scent.)

The path roller-coasters up and down the steep sides of the glen. Sometimes you can see the water tumbling over rock ledges or resting in shallow pools. There are few loose rocks in the stream bed because they have tumbled down stream during spring floods when the water has literally moved mountains down into Cayuga Lake.

The continuing rippling and gurgling of water, tall trees, bright spots of sunlight dappling through the trees on the water make a restful, peaceful setting. It is the timelessness of it that makes it secure and serene. I feel no need to hurry and would like to capture this moment to be treasured again and again in some future time of need.

***

The glen abruptly turns into a gaping rock crevasse with walls three hundred feet high. Even the maples are gone from the sides of the stream. The path merges with the shale-like layered steep walls and it takes a moment to adjust from the dark forest to the bright sun reflecting off the glaring, noisy, ground-trembling, high-falling Lucifer Falls. Pictures cannot capture the enormous power of the water here.

Now the trail becomes a series of steps climbing through the rock crevasse. Workmen are cementing the thick stone fence where winter storm waters washed it out. The materials are let down to the workmen on a cable from the opposite side where there is an overlook from the Rim Trail. Although the FLT doesn't go near the gorge, there are directions in the

trail booklet for taking a side trip to the overlook, using other park trails.

It looks like the workers have a continuous job of repairing to do. All along the trail is a waist high stone slab wall that has been cemented in place. The stone looks like it has come from the stream bed. It is a work of art in itself and I wager it goes unnoticed because it seems to be a natural part of the gorge. After seeing the immensity of the glen and the amount of upkeep that is necessary, I don't feel the overnight fee is expensive at all. It would be easy to spend days getting acquainted with the pools, moods of the forest and different rock formations.

A young couple carrying a baby in a sling baby-tender passed me enthusiastically shortly after I started and I met them returning not long afterward. I doubt if they got this far and they don't know what they missed.

There are some places where the trail would be nonexistent when the water gets high. In one area the trail is almost level with the stream. Branches, twigs and other debris are tangled in the grass and shrubs several feet beyond the trail. Clumps of long slender leaves of day lilies form a nearly continuous low green fence along the trail. In season it would be a nodding orange fence. We call them Fourth of July Flowers, because that's about the time they start blooming. The unopen buds make a tasty snack for hikers. The morning mist has cleared now and the sky is a bright cloudless blue.

I meet a group of people coming down from the Upper Park as I reach a wide cove. It's amazing the things people wear on their feet for an outing. They wear zories and street shoes. With this kind of trail, good-fitting sneakers would be fine and not weigh as much as these hiking boots, but there are places on the trail where it would be hard not to walk in the mud or through a puddle. The trail starts at four-hundred fifty feet above sea level at the Lower Park and rises to one thousand fifty feet at the Upper Park.

Too soon, I'm in the Upper Park where the water is a gurgling small stream, except in one place where there is an old grain mill. It was built in 1839 and worked until 1917.

The mill is a monument to man's use of natural water power. The inside of the building has been fixed to allow people to tour through. The two grinding stones are not as large as I expected, less than four feet in diameter, but I wouldn't want to try to lift one stone even a little bit.

Downstairs are the wooden gears and shafts that the water wheel turned to transfer the energy to moving the stones. It is an elaborate job of engineering and craftsmanship to actually carve the pieces of wood for the notched gears and wheels. It would be very difficult if not impossible to make any wooden ones like them today.

I wonder if we have given up more than we have gained with our man-made materials.

Even though there are picnic areas in the Upper Park, I choose to have lunch along the stream part way back down the glen. It is too hot in the direct sun and there is a place below the falls where water runs over a flat area and under some overhanging maple trees. It is a nice place to sit and it is cooling to listen to the water gurgling over the little steps and be cooled by the breeze. It's tempting to wade or at least let the water wash over my feet, but I'm not sure I'd be able to get my boots on properly again.

There are many more people on the trail now and the sun's angle has changed from this morning making the path and glen look much different.

It doesn't seem like this small amount of water could support much life but both the water and the area around it is teeming with life. Most noticeable are the spider webs as the sun glistens off their four times stronger-than-steel silk traps. I see a fly struggling in a web which may be made from three or four kinds of silk. The Orb Weaver, maker of this silk trap, has several different silk glands. The silk is extruded from its spinnerets under its abdomen, and can produce either dragline silk, that allows them to drift with the air currents; sticky threads, that captured the fly; another for wrapping the fly for another day's meal; reinforcing threads for the web, and thread for cocoons.

However what often appears to us as gory when a predator (we are predators too) kills its prey, in actuality the pain we imagine the creature to suffer is not felt as the shock of it masks the initial pain.

Mankind has effected all creatures in one way or another, and is this very moment, destroying the environmental ingredients that creatures need to survive.

It is now necessary for man to try to balance what he has done with wildlife management. We have eliminated the larger predators and rather than have surpluses die of starvation or disease, we manage the surplus of declared game animals by harvesting, just as the farmer sells his animals to the market place and keeps a brood stock.

We are made of the same basic materials as all other life on this earth and are dependent upon it for our life, if we don't recognize the interdependence and natures' cycle of death and birth we are liable to wake up some day and find we have destroyed it.

* * *

There aren't any big fish in the stream, but there are thousands of microscopic creatures that are the base of many food chains. There are crayfish that look like miniature lobsters, worms, centipedes and salamanders hiding under rocks that live on the microscopic food. Toads visit the quiet pools in the spring to lay eggs, a coal skink, might hide under debris in the water by day and forage for food at night. A water snake might come looking for a dinner of crayfish, worms or beetles. A variety of birds dine on backswimmers, water striders, dragonfly nymphs, or even on caddisfly larva carrying its own distinctive tube house made of wood, leaves, sand or even silk with them as they look for food. Bats swoop and cut the air eating mosquitos, stoneflies and other flying insects at night. Raccoons poke about in the stream with their hand like paws looking for a dinner of crayfish.

In the cool hours shrews scurry along the banks looking for insects, worms, snails and young mice. A shrew is the only mammal in the United States that has poisonous saliva. Because its metabolism rate is so high it must eat more than its own weight each day to survive. Sparrows, warblers, catbirds, hawks, jays, crows, chickadees, swallows, woodpeckers, nighthawks, owls, grouse and phoebe live in the woods along the stream and feed on the insects, berries and small animals.

Although you can't always see the animals that visit here it is possible to see the signs they have left. Besides footprints in the mud or sand left by raccoons, opossums, birds, worms, there is the silvery mucus trail of a snail and the seed-like droppings of a mouse. Getting to know an area intimately takes time, patience and alert senses.

Skunk, weasel, grey fox, bobcat, squirrel, turkey, porcupine and deer come to the water to drink or search for food. Mice and voles must always be on the lookout for predators as they search for seeds, grass and berries. The stream is a busy place and clean water unpolluted by man's chemicals is the foundation of life in the glen.

Water striders skating on the water make thin ripples on the standing pools of water. With the sun at your back and looking below the trees and shrubs over the water, you can see spiders' silken lines floating in the breeze. There are bees, flies and smaller insects buzzing and droning in their particular band of air above the earth. Some are creeping, some jumping, some flitting in the endless cycle of making more of their kind and providing for another new generation.

There aren't many territorial bird songs sung this month. All the parents are tired or still fetching food for their bottomless youngsters. One of the seasons' last birds to nest is the colorful yellow and black goldfinch, because some of their favorite foods, dandelion and thistle seeds are not mature until now. They prefer to line their nest within the thick foliage of a shrub with powder-soft thistle down.

When I arrive back in camp I feel stump-legged. Obviously not at all in condition. It is much easier walking down hill but I must have given other muscles a good work out. The steep cliff was not as scary and high coming back, I think it is because there was more sun on the path and I had proven to myself that it could be walked without falling over the edge.

* * *

After rinsing out some clothes, enjoying a quick swim and packing the chair and bike in the van, I head toward Buttermilk Falls State Park and the city of Ithaca.

I am puzzled because I almost immediately enter the outskirts of Ithaca on Route 13. Most parks are not within the city limits. I must be going in the wrong direction.

Unable to resist a plaza, I find a book, a pair of knee high stockings for boot liners and almost leave the store without making any purchase because there's such a long line for one cashier.

Then I see a combination store and hope it will be my chance to get another sleeping pad so I can backpack. Wandering around in the store I find some sneakers on sale that might work better if the trails at Buttermilk are as good as the trails at Treman. The store has air mattresses but they don't work for me because they press on a tender kidney. Next door is a grocery store where, while looking for a small salt shaker because I did not bring enough, I pick up an appetizing small steak that's on sale.

The clerk said that Buttermilk Falls is back down the highway about two blocks. It isn't any more than a mile and a half from Treman to Buttermilk! They both run into Cayuga Inlet that empties into Cayuga Lake.

The FLT runs from Robert Treman 1.7 miles to a spur trail that is about 1.5 miles long that goes to the upper part of Buttermilk Falls. The FLT maps numbers 16 and 17 show the two trails. Although the FLT doesn't actually go by the falls in either park it does go by one of the many other scenic falls of the area called Lick Brook Gorge.

Other scenic streams in the area are Cascadilla Glen, Fall Creek and Six Mile Creek. All feed into Cayuga Inlet then Cayuga Lake and are within Ithaca's city limits.

Ithaca is credited with the invention of the ice cream sundae. The person probably got the idea from the buildings perched on top of one of the seven hills of Ithaca one winter day. The tall Clinton Billared House in downtown Ithaca, just off Buffalo on Tioga Street and next to DeWitte Park is the place to go for tours of the city.

Back up into the watershed of Cayuga Lake south off Route 13 near Newfield about six miles from here is the Newfield Bridge. Built in 1853, at a cost of $800, it is one of the 25 authentic covered bridges in New York State.

It is easy to see why they call the falls Buttermilk Falls. The way the water cascades down the slightly increasing curved rock it looks like an old fashion ball gown, bubbling and picking up the air, making it look like milk pouring down over the rocks.

The Park's main gate, at the foot of the falls, is 400 feet above sea level and the upper part of the Park is 1,000 feet. Buttermilk was also given to the state by Mr. and Mrs. Treman in 1924 and was added to until it now covers 751 acres. Like other state parks in New York, there are special passes available for unlimited use for senior citizens and for permanently disabled people.

The camping area is halfway up a very steep hill on the opposite side of the valley from Treman. After registering for site number 38, I study the park map. The camping area is limited to a flat area on the side of the steep hillside. Because it is a popular campground I doubt if it will be easy to find wood though only one-third of the sites are occupied now.

Talk about coincidence, both my older boys are working in the kitchen of a summer camp and guess which camp happens to have a group camping here? Now the rest of the family will know where I am by the grapevine. See, you are never really alone.

My space, back up against a hill again, is about as far from the entrance as it can be and hopefully it is close to any available wood supply. Wrong again, the hill is steep and has been cleared of any obvious wood laying on the ground. An old stacked stone fence runs diagonally up the hill in back of me, maybe there is wood on the other side of it.

There is a continuous drone and vibration from the highway traffic, at least it is a little ways away, besides it's the rush hour. Tomorrow I'll be somewhere else. It's much too hot to start anything strenuous or involved so I'll read for awhile.

* * *

Later, while looking for wood, the only thing I find after climbing a long distance is a large patch of poison ivy and I'm in the middle of it. The park must have had a busy summer, the only wood I find is a couple of small dead sumac branches. They are from the Staghorn Sumac plant that can grow up to the size of a small tree. We call Staghorn Sumac because it resembles the antlers of a stag when in velvet. It is a common plant that has bright red tight cone shaped clusters of berries with small hairs. A sour pink refreshing drink can be made by simmering the berries, straining the juice to remove the hairs and adding a sweetener.

Ninety-four different kinds of birds including the ruffed grouse and pheasant eat the berries because they stay on the sumac into the winter. Rabbits particularly like the tender bark and last year's snow line can be estimated by the light rings left after the bark is eaten. Deer eat sumac in the summer and autumn and it is one of the main sources of food in the winter.

The sumac is a member of the cashew family who's sister plant in Japan has ink made from the sap. If you cut a twig the white sap will soon turn black on the knife blade because it contains tannin. Old time trappers used to boil their traps in a solution of sumac and walnut hulls to protect them from rusting and to give them a natural odor. The Native Americans used the split bark in basket weaving and for stomach aches. The roots were used for yellow dye. They used the crushed leaves as a poultice for skin diseases.

Sumac is one of the first plants to turn scarlet red in the fall and is found in dry areas. Beware of poison sumac that grows in moist places, it has leaflets that are smooth on the margin, are NOT silvery beneath and has a CLEAR juice that turns black when dry. Poison sumac has the same potential for allergic reactions as does poison ivy, also a member of the cashew_family.

What made the wood hunting excursion up the mountain interesting is the hill is all shale with hardly any soil. The shale is in paper thin sheets and it is impossible not to break it as you walk. Every time you take a step it sounds like you are walking on and breaking ceramic plates. The crunching cracking sound is hard to get use to. Shale is formed from clay deposits that have been subject to pressure and heat and if enough heat and pressure is applied to the shale it will turn to slate.

It took several climbs up the slippery shale_beyond the stone fence to get enough branches for a fire. Later I noticed next to my tumble down fireplace, in the middle of a heap of brush and brambles a nice big dead branch. Not passing up an opportunity for easy wood, I drag it out and leave it near the fireplace. When I start stacking the wood I look at the brush pile again and realize that it is also a poison ivy patch. Very carefully I push the branch back away from the other wood, glad that I noticed the poison ivy before I started breaking the wood up.

There are not many people at the park, but after one of my longer trips for wood I find a note under my orange coffee cup on the picnic table. It is from a Camper's Assistance Program representative. It said, "Welcome campers!" We hope your stay here is the best ever! We're here to help you make the most of your camping experience. As volunteers in the state wide Camper Assistance Program (CAP), Sponsored by the New York State office of Parks Recreation and Historic Preservation, we are experienced campers familiar with the park and surrounding region. We're available to help you: get settled at your site, bring "uncooperative" equipment under control, learn about activities that are yours to enjoy in the park, become familiar with services and things to do or see nearby, keep the campground in good order, help resolve questions and problems that might arise...or just sit and chat, recalling camping adventures. You can find us at the site with the CAP sign. Our bright red caps or scarves and buttons will help you to recognize us. Drop by and say hello. We're here to help, and we're looking forward to meeting you. Your CAP Volunteers Site #28". I've never heard of CAP before but it sounds like a good idea.

***

A man in his early twenties drives a small car in to a campsite across the road from me. He takes down a bicycle from top of the car. Then he sets up a tan dome tent, gets back in the car and drives off.

Next a Volkswagon pulls into the site opposite me and an older man dressed in a suit gets out, pulls out a lawn chair, puts a briefcase on the table and starts to read a newspaper. He appears to be a commuting salesman.

Later, an older couple comes strolling by and stop to talk to the salesman and I cannot help but overhear some of the conversation. He speaks with a heavy German accent but I don't get a clue as to what he is doing here. From the way they are talking both have been camping in the park for at least several days.

The woman is telling the salesman, "I can't believe how windy it is by our campsite. We are afraid to start a fire tonight. We don't want to catch the woods afire."

"You should be here on this side, there is little wind here."

"It must be the wind is from the north, and it comes

around the mountain," the woman says and they continue to discuss the wind.

The white haired couple in pastel clothes seem to be bored with their evening routine.

Right next to the trees behind my fireplace and mixed with the ivy is a berry bush with a leaf that looks like a maple leaf and has small white flowers with yellow centers. I try to add to the list of plants that I can identify whenever possible and in order to do this I have a small library of field guides that I try to remember to bring when I go on a trip.

Different authors have varied approaches to identification. Some books are for the novice and very general while others are scientific. Usually between a couple of them it is possible to find something that looks reasonably like what's been found. It helps to have guide books that are limited to your particular area because that makes finding the name a little easier.

According to the books, there are over 200 varieties of the Rubis or Prickly Brambles family, this bush is either a Canadian Black Current, Rock Gooseberry or a Thimbleberry bramble. All berries have more vitamin C when fresh than an orange and all kinds of creatures, from chipmunks, to birds and bears eat them. It is possible that this is an escapee from the Cornell Botanical Gardens via the droppings of any one of the 150 kinds of birds that eat berries.

Because my legs are still rubbery and my hip sore, further exploring of trails can wait until tomorrow. It was stupid to sleep on the knife. It's a good example of how a stupid mistake can get a person into an awkward position and allows friend Murphy to come calling with an accident.

No tent tonight, the plastic pegs won't go into the shale. That's what I should have gotten at a store; long nails! The book I bought was Sacajawea, the story of the Native American girl that helped Lewis and Clark on their expedition west. It is appropriate for this region, but it is the wrong tribe. I should read about Hiawatha, or Red Jacket. Red Jacket_was born near the northern end of Seneca Lake and was a great

orator. He was used as an interpreter and is said by some historical white authors to have been two-faced. How you interpret his life depends on whether you are trying to open up new territory or keep your own land. The Seneca Chief's name came from a red jacket presented to him by the British at Fort Niagara when he was a messenger for them during the Revolution. Later on, after he had established his reputation he went to Philadelphia and spoke with President Washington as a representative of the Iroquois.

***

The grill in the van was put to use over the crumbling fireplace and my sumac fire doesn't burn very well.

Ash wood is the best for camp fires and will even burn when green if necessary. The ash trees are members of the Olive Family, although their fruit is usually winged unlike the Olive tree. Ash wood is used for tool handles, baseball bats, tennis rackets, skis and oars. Live trees should never be cut for campfires in parks.

It would have been helpful to have a hatchet, not to cut wood but to pound in tent stakes. The small bow saw would be more than adequate for cutting the small wood if it were sharp. It would be good to learn how to sharpen it and would be something for me to do around a camp fire. (Why didn't I think to try it with my special knife?)

The campsite is out in the open and close to the road and it seems that the circling evening strollers slow down as they pass by.

There's not the usual quieting of noise and activity from the group from the summer camp; instead their singing volume increases with the size of their bonfire.

As I gaze into the flickering flames of my own fire and try to shut out the surrounding sounds, I find my mind wandering. The cool night and warm fire are not normal parts of my every day living, and as I experience it, I wonder if anyone knows where I am. I become suspicious that I may not even be where I think I am.

I recall a cool spring night a year ago when my husband and I were traveling near this very spot. We were looking for a short-cut that would take us down the hillside to the brightly lit highway we could see below us.

After turning off a four lane highway toward the valley, we drove a couple of miles down the hill on a narrow winding unlit country road. We made one left and one right turn, always heading downhill. After a long time, we thought we should be coming to the intended valley road and saw a four lane highway before us. We were flabbergasted to discover that we had come back to the original highway about an eighth of a mile up the hill from where we had turned off.

Thank goodness we didn't have any breakdowns or flats on our short cut, where ever we had been, because there is no telling what might have happened or where we would be today.

Even in the light of day, after studying two maps while driving over the same four-lane highway, we were at a complete loss to explain how we had accomplished such a maneuver without crossing any main roads or going over any bridges and still ended up coming <u>down</u> a hill we had never gone <u>up.</u> The incident made me wonder if such an experience started area native Rod Serling on his career writing the "Twilight Zone".

***

The mosquitos are not bad tonight so the windows are left open while I have the last cup of coffee. Some of the more persistent bugs find their way under the netting that is held around the open windows by magnets. The nylon netting and magnets are easy to store and usually allow a window to be open to let the air circulate. This system doesn't require any special work to be done on the van and is easy to store.

It takes a few seconds to connect the rustling I hear next to the van with the earlier slowing of bike riders looking for wood. They are taking the wood from the clump of brush, but good grief, they will have pulled it through the poison ivy.

Moments later there is a slight whiff of smoke in the van and I scramble to close the windows tightly, saying a prayer for the rustlers and for the campers that are next to the fire, that there will not be any poison ivy on the wood.

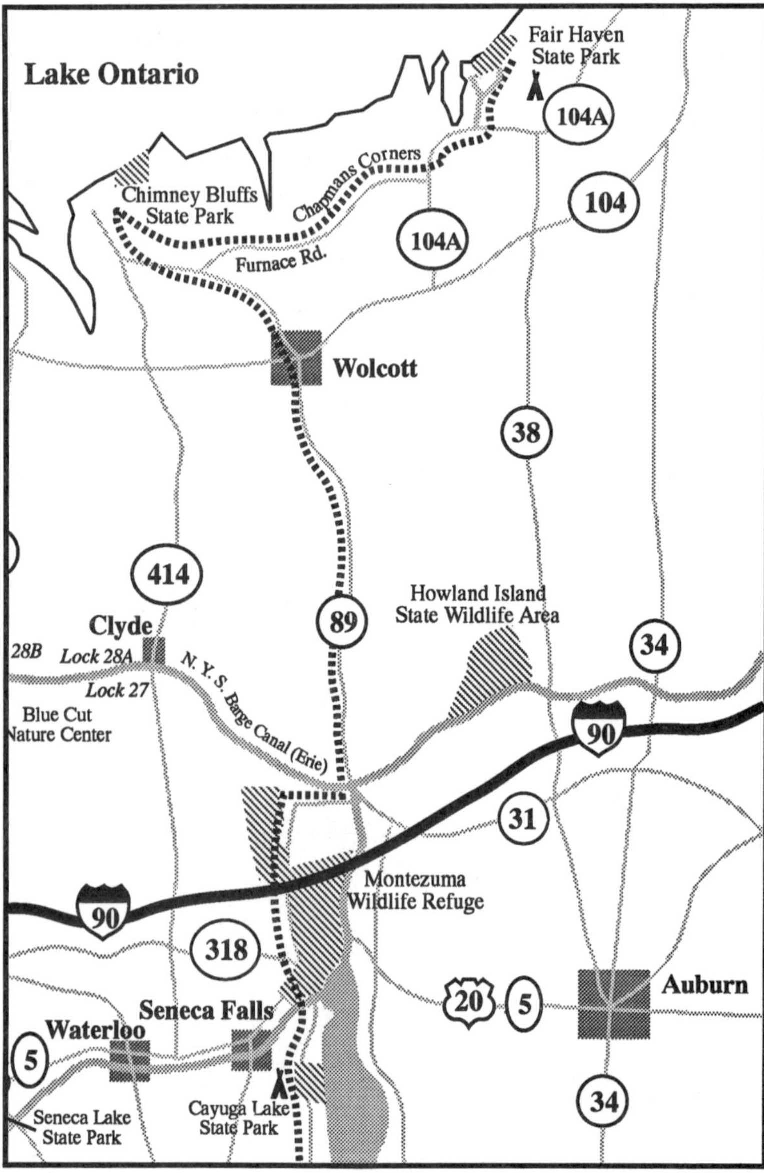

(Southern section of Map on Page 92)

Lake to the Horizon
(Northern Section)

LAKE IN A BOWL
&
LAKE TO THE HORIZON

Bless the Lord, my soul: Oh Lord my God,
thou art great indeed.
Thou dost make springs break out in the gullies
so that their water runs between the hills.
Psalm 104 vs 1 & 10

It is going to be a nice day, the air is clear and the sky crisp and blue. Sunrise is happening on the other side of the hill and won't be here for awhile. The morning rush-hour traffic is in full roar on Route 13 below. Not wanting to look for more wood or try a fire, I use the gas stove to heat water for cereal. I'm surprised that the ice has held out so well in the cooler. Frozen gallon containers of water work very well and are not nearly as messy as the plastic bags of ice. Why don't they make larger containers to put the ice in so it won't melt all over and float the food in the cold water? All the coolers seem to be odd sizes and none have any way of holding the bagged ice so the food doesn't become waterlogged. Cheese and butter lose something after they've been floating in a combination of ice water, pickle juice, hot dogs and milk.

The salesman has left, the student isn't stirring yet: there is hope and newness to the day as the dew dries. As the light becomes stronger the birds seem more cheerful.

The trail for today starts at the entrance of the Park so I pack up, drive to the parking lot and put on a little pack sack. Starting up hill gets the hard part out of the way first.

The North Rim Trail doesn't waste any time going up and up along the edge of the gorge; in some places it is on a ridge and in others on the edge of the gorge.

Once the trail is away from the road, the woods are cool and church quiet, aside from the birds singing. The trail starts on the shady side of the hill but as it goes higher the sunlight streams through the tops of the trees lighting up other trees like spot lights. As the light increases the birds get noisier and more active and there seem to be birds in every tree and on the trail every fifteen feet.

The rim trail divides at a sign that points to an Overlook. The rim is peaceful as the new day's sunlight streams through the trees, but the path toward the dark gorge and water looks more inviting and mysterious.

Each gorge has its own personality. This stream likes to carve out nearly perfect round potholes at the bottom of almost every falls. The water is so clear it is hard to determine how deep the hole is, even with its slight greenish tinge. Some holes look like they are a foot or so below the stream bed while others look like they might be eight to ten feet deep. I take some pictures but if it fools the eye, how can it be captured on film?

One hole has many egg shaped rocks that have ground around in the hole for eons as the water swirls down and around pushing the rocks around and around slowly wearing away the walls. The newer rocks are basketball size and it must take considerable force to make them move. None are moving today, at least they don't appear to be.

The water is so clear it is hard to see that it is even moving except where it ripples over the flat places like steps, falls off the ledges, or rushes between huge rocks. In some places the stream bed has faulted so perfectly, it looks like it was cut or stacked by man. The square sharp right angle corners contrast to the worn round potholes.

The layered shale walls are not as high as in Treman's State Park. Trees seem to be hanging on the edges with claw like roots. Roots that have forced themselves into the rocks, split them and caused pieces to fall into the water. The trees must have other roots deep into the walls because they have grown to full size. As I walk along I expect to witness a tree falling into the gully at the next curve. The permanence of the trees and walls is assured where mats of moss are growing thick and ferns gently tap the wall in the breeze.

There are three-hundred varieties of ferns in the United States and they range in size from less than an inch to tree size. The fern's stems and roots are underground. Their leaves are called frons. Ancient ferns supplied some of the vegetable matter which later formed the great coal deposits in Pennsylvania. Nowhere on earth are there comparable places where new coal fields are being formed in huge swampy areas.

In the Middle ages in Europe, ferns were avoided because people thought they had the power of making things invisible. They couldn't see the fern seeds, which are microscopic size spores so they thought they were invisible.

The bracken fern produces a chemical defense that makes it toxic to cows, deer, raccoons, mice and opossums. It also produces a large amount of insect growth hormone which confuses the development of insects feeding on the plant. The unpleasant odor and waving motion of a couple of ferns stuck in a hat band helps keep away pesky bugs.

A moss tapestry grows abundantly in the shady, cool and moist gorge. It actually grows in two different stages. One stage produces tiny spores that produce a plant that reproduces by flower fertilization.

Mosses are soil makers. They break off tiny bits of rock with their roots and their leaves gather dust from the air. This way of making soil is a very slow process. Moss plays an important part in the water holding ability of the forest and helps prevent flooding. By holding the water it provides a more continuous supply of run-off for streams. Examination with a hand lens reveals a miniature world in the moss, complete with an assortment of monster-like bugs.

Water oozing through the soil and maze of rocks finds freedom at the edge of the gorge rock wall and drips onto the path. In the winter it is a white ice fairyland when the water freezes as it hits the cold air and makes marble ice statues.

When water freezes it expands and exerts tremendous forces which can break huge rocks apart. There must be an impressive amount of clean up necessary in the spring from the slides caused by the ice breaking the rocks. For safety, all of the State Park gorges are closed in the winter and early spring while other parts of some of the parks remain open for snowmobiles, cross country skiing and other activities.

The walk through the gorge seems timeless, particularly because I haven't met any one else. Unexpectedly, the trail comes to a highway bridge and narrows to a set of stairs to climb up to a road.

The West King Road crosses the glen here and can be taken to get access to the FLT. According to the Park map I will have climbed nearly 600 feet after I get to the high side of a lake that should be around here somewhere. The Upper Park has large mowed lawns and open places following the road which winds with the quiet little stream into the woods.

I am not ready for the end of the walk nor ready to see the noisy people who appear on the stairs, heading down the trail. Following the stream I can see a wooden dam that has been completely filled in with large rocks, trees and trash. It is a good example of how a dam slows the water, which makes the water drop whatever it has been carrying along. It is an inevitable law of dams that eventually they will be filled in from behind and therefore hold less water back. As farming practices are becoming more intense again, and there is more erosion of farm land (a national problem now), the fill-in happens faster. Dams constructed for the purpose of containing flood waters will have to be dredged out from time to time or new dams will have to be built.

Further up the stream, where the woods grow closer to the water, is a small cement dam, five feet or so high and about ten feet wide. Children from a day camp are sitting along the edge fishing. None of the children seem to have fished before nor are they getting any bites from the weedy coffee with cream water. They look like they have had enough fishing and are trying to get one another wet by dipping the tips of their rods into the water and shaking them at each other. The counselor looks like he is trying to figure out what he will do with the children for the rest of the time allotted.

The trail goes over the small cement dam to the other side of a tall rock formation. Stairs go up the side, around the face and to the far side where it is possible to see the whole of Robert Treman Lake. It looks like a bowl surrounded by trees, but surprise, the other side of the rock pile is not the same, it is a sheer, deep gully with a large curved stone dam about 100 feet wide holding back the lake.

The dam is made from large grey-blue stones with rounded faces, laid up like brick. It is semicircular and goes from the rock just climbed over to a rock face on the other side.

From the floor of the gully to the top of the slightly slanted dam face is about 45 feet. There is a pipe and wire fence on the gully side with a four foot walkway over the dam. With water lapping at the walkway it doesn't seem that the narrow dam could hold back so much water.

Not only is the size of the dam a surprise but there are people climbing up the dam wall! Several college age teachers are teaching high school students mountain climbing. According to one of the young instructors, it is a Physical Education Course offered by Cornell to high school students.

The teachers are methodical in their instructions to the students as to where to place their hands and feet and remembering the safety rules. It appears the best part of the lessons comes when the students repel back down to the bottom. They slip down the line and spring back off the stones with their feet. Each team keeps constant track of each other, their lines and what they are doing. My legs become weak and my heart goes to my mouth just watching them.

Once on the other side of the dam, the path goes around the rock face and up a steep ridge. The lake is like a tree green bowl filled with water. I wonder where the stream is that feeds it? The trees surrounding it are a mixture of maple, oak

and hemlock trees. Rows of pine trees in some places show that they were planted. The banks all around seem to be steep except where the water flows out and the children are fishing.

Looking at the map again shows why I am having trouble with my sense of direction. The trail goes south, contradicting the usual direction of water. Flowing north doesn't seem right, although it often occurs in the Finger Lakes.

The path forks and I take the trail continuing around the lake. The other fork is the spur that intersects with the FLT and Robert Treman State Park. The ground becomes flatter as the trail approaches the half-way mark and crosses a small stream that hardly seems large enough to provide the amount of water rushing down the gorge. There must be springs that feed the main stream too.

Not far on in the woods is a low moist place, (probably from a spring), and a dark log Adirondack lean-to. It is cave-like inside because it is in a shaded depression.

As I come around the corner to step inside, a barn owl silently rushes out the other side, startling both of us. It must have been roosting on one the beams. There are log benches all the way around the inside walls and visitors have left them pock-marked with engravings.

The rounded log bench retains the cold from last night as I sit and speculate on the people and activities that might have been here. There is not much of a view, but the nearby swampy area sends the aroma of skunk cabbage and muck over to me. An early flower of spring, the skunk cabbage is one of the plants that grows a protective leaf that covers its flower. Native American remedies used the dried leaves in a concoction including molasses and honey for coughs and a mixture of garlic and other herbs for the relief of bronchial asthma. The smell is moist, cool and clean with just a hint of skunk cabbage smell. The odors here are much different from the smells of the gorge.

A squirrel peeks through a sunlit hole in the roof near the outer part of the overhang, gives a shriek, jerks his tail and chucks at me angrily for intruding. He's lucky it is me he discovers and not the owl or he would be the owl's lunch.

There isn't any other person here, but I have the feeling there are others present, perhaps because this gorge was once a meeting place for the Cayuga Indians.

Three-quarters of the way around the lake I meet a group of children whooping and hollering like a bunch of wild Indians as they race around the lake. It's not likely that real Native Americans would ever make this much noise. I wonder if the lake was a swamp or a lake when the Native Americans lived here. They probably didn't have such nice trails to walk on, or did they? My legs have stiffened from sitting so long on the cold wood and it takes several minutes of walking to get them working right again.

The warm sun feels good as I arrive at the small dam. A different group of children are fishing, but they seem more interested in sitting on the bank and talking or checking out the underside of the rocks in a small rivulet feeding the lake.

There are many more people in the park now, including a group of senior citizens who have arrived by bus. They seem more enthusiastic than the children. The large mowed fields along the stream can accommodate several groups. Children at a double picnic table are busy weaving a "nature" wall hanging with yarn and things they have found on a previous walk.

The trail back to the gorge looks interesting and not as busy as the road route and I have it all to myself. It is a pleasant trail with many of the tall trees blown down here too, like a giant had swung his hand and knocked them all over in the same direction.

The main gorge trail holds an unexplained magnetism, so instead of taking the rim trail back I pick the water way. Four people are wading up the middle of the stream where it is mostly flat. It's not a good idea because there is moss growing on the rocks and it makes them slippery, but it looks like fun!

Part way back down there is a rock formation standing in the bottom of the glen called Pinnacle Rock. It is almost as high as the walls of the gorge. Eons ago this rock must have been just a little harder than the surrounding rock and the fall of the water went around the rock. As time passed the water washed away the surrounding stone, leaving the small island which even has a tree growing on it. Not more than six feet square, it is near the west side of the wall and seems far enough back from the stream now that it will probably survive an eon more.

Everyone should visit at least one of these places of creation. Photographs cannot show the carvings of the water in full perspective. Although the sound might be captured, the soft breezes, moist air, smell of moss and feeling of isolation from the cares of the world cannot be captured except by the soul. It's no wonder the gorge was used for the filming of the Perils of Pauline in the early days of film making.

I pick a spot in the sun looking over a series of falls and a kettlehole to eat lunch. The sneakers with two pairs of socks have worked out so far. I'm glad I didn't have to lug around the heavy hiking boots this time. The cooler walking makes a difference in how thirsty you get.

A ten year old boy runs full speed past me on the way to the top. About half an hour later a concerned mother and younger sister come panting up the stairs and ask if I've seen a boy with blue shorts. She explains she was careful to give him specific directions not to go too far ahead. Obviously the boy felt challenged to get to the top first. How far is "ahead" when you are the fearless leader, the explorer, or the adventurer?

On part of the gorge trail I missed this morning, there is a stretch so narrow a person couldn't fit in the crack that the water has to flow through. The rock walls are only about six feet wide and the water has to knife through a narrow cut only about a foot wide. I can't see how deep the crack is. The whole width of the gorge at this point must be about 12 feet. It's a wonder that such a narrow spot can exist so far down the gorge when high water must exert so much pressure and the debris should wear the walls away.

The extreme width of the gorge is only a few yards down stream, where there is a gaping amphitheater where the water has eaten the soft rocks away. Buttermilk Falls is below it.

There are a few people swimming in the green marked off pool below the falls. A cool breeze is blowing up the valley from Cayuga Lake and the water doesn't look inviting right now, so I watch the swimmers from a shaded picnic table. The retrieved thermos from the van holds down the corner of the map so the next destination can be decided.

* * *

Decisions, decisions: west to Watkins Glen State Park or east to Fillmore. I'd rather go somewhere I haven't been before.

Fillmore Glen State Park named after the former President born nearby, is about twenty-four miles northeast of Ithaca outside Moravia, which is known for its annual bathtub races in July. Fillmore Glen is always nice and cool in the summer and there is some sort of interesting program almost every night. Long Point State Park on the east side of Cayuga Lake is about thirty miles north from here and just south of Aurora.

I'll try north on Route 89 to Cayuga Lake State Park on the west shore of the Lake. Part way up toward the park opposite Romulus on Vineyard Road is Misty Meadow, where for a small fee you can have the grand tour of a modern day hog farm, snack at their pavilion, visit their store, get some free recipes, see how our pork is raised and even have a hayride.

Frontenac Island, north of Long Point State Park, is a rare island of the Finger Lakes. It is about seven miles from the northern end of Cayuga Lake and west of Union Springs. The island, about an acre in size, is the remains of a coral reef from the Paleozoic Era.

There is a theory that the very first inhabitants of this area came by way of the Bering Sea about five thousand years ago. Their way of life is referred to as the Lamokan Culture because of the discovery of them near Lamoka Lake. The first people probably lived on the island during the summer around two-thousand BC. Archaeologists determined from graves found on the island that the pre-woodland people ate deer, bear, elk, and some raccoons, aquatic animals and birds. They made fire by striking flint to get a spark and had bone flutes and rattles made with turtle shells and small white pebbles. It would be interesting to sit around one of their camp fires and listen to their songs.

Pottery, smoking pipes, cultivation of corn, beans and squash didn't occur until around one thousand BC. The Iroquois developed from the Woodland Culture but didn't form the League of Nations until the 1600's. In 1772 the Tuscoras were the 6th and last to join the Iroquois Confederacy.

The Native Americans became upset when the colonists began taking land along the Mohawk and Susquehanna River and retaliated by killing the settlers. They did not understand the white's idea of land ownership, feeling that land existed for all people as they needed its resources.

One of the villages destroyed as the Sullivan expedition marched northwest was at the base of Buttermilk Falls. Another village destroyed was a mile or so south of Sampson State Park on the east side of Seneca Lake somewhere near the Boy Scout Camp of Babcock Hovey. Sullivan also destroyed Kanadesage, the Native American Capital located west of Geneva toward Seneca Castle. The path of destruction included the village of Queen Catherine near Montour Falls, Kashong on the northwest side of Seneca Lake and Skanqartenate at the head of Canandaigua Lake.

* * *

Cayuga Lake State Park is a nicely planned 185 acre park that has been described as the most beautiful park in Central New York. There are lots of shade trees with level camping, a nice beach for swimming and a boat launch for fishing, water skiing or the new sport of sail flying. Cayuga Lake State Park has a Winter Festival with ice fishing contests, cross country skiing, snow shoeing, other contests and displays.

As I pass by it looks like there are many others enjoying the park and I'm ready for some wide open spaces. The ocean is too far away in time and money but the next best thing to

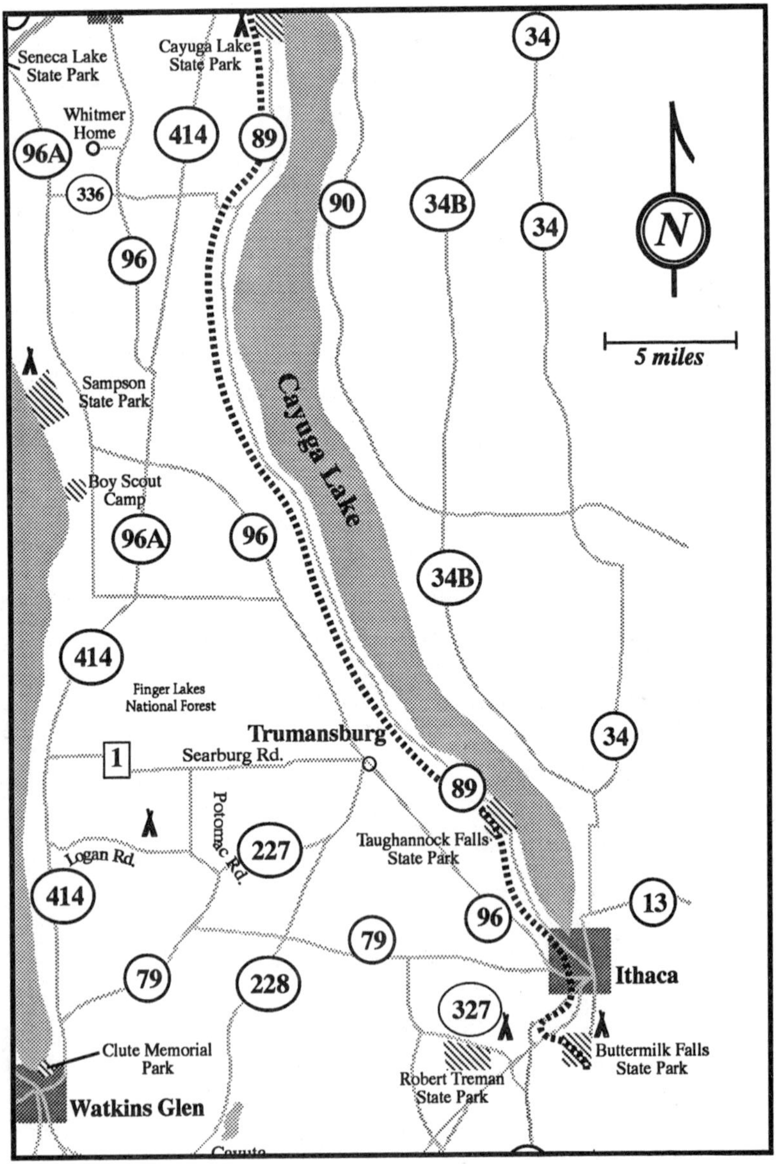

(Northern section of Map on Page 80)

Lake to the Horizon
(Southern Section)

an ocean is the sandy beaches of the Great Lakes, Lake Ontario, and it is only about thirty miles away.

Route 89 is not a main artery but it is in good repair, scenic and has little traffic. It runs through Montezeuma National Wildlife Refuge which is operated by the Department of the Interior. The Clyde River/Erie Canal are the boundaries on the north and the Seneca River/Seneca Canal are boundaries on the south and east.

The main entrance to Montezuma is on Route 5 and 20 which runs through the southern section of the park. That road comes from Geneva and goes to the city of Auburn about twelve miles to the east, and north of Owasco Lake.

Montezuma with its waves of wind blown cattails got its name from its similarity to the plains of Mexico. The refuge includes a marshy area twelve miles long and eight miles wide. It is one of the most productive wetlands in North America and was established in 1936 when the marsh was restored after an unsuccessful attempt to drain it for farming.

Three hundred-fourteen species of birds have been identified in the refuge since 1937. Some are migratory, others nest here. Forty-four species of waterfowl, song birds, and shore birds rarely seen have been identified. This is partly due to the Refuge being in the fringe of their territory, while others have been blown off course. Some are victims of man changing their environment, either in the United States or South America where many spend the winter. Changing weather patterns have also moved the birds to different territories.

Some birds are rare because their special food has been limited or their nesting sites destroyed. The purple house finch is an example of a newcomer to this region from the south. Another seventy-four species have been identified by at least one of the many enthusiastic bird watchers who flock to the refuge, especially during migrating times.

Wetlands help to reduce flooding. They slow the water down and act like a sponge. Wetlands clean the water too. Heavy particles of soil drop to the bottom and the plants use up the extra nutrients as well as absorbing pollutants. Cattails may someday be used to separate pollutants from water.

Wetlands are a nursery for many creatures that get their start in life in the marsh and then move to open water. Wetlands are oxygen makers too. They provide food and cover for a whole system of interdependent plants, insects, animals, fish and birds, some of which we depend on. Of the limited number of acres of our national wetlands that we have, over 1,200 more acres are being permanently filled in EVERY DAY and we are experiencing NOW, shortages of marine life because of it. And that doesn't even include what we're destroying because of pollution.

* * *

Due to the invasion of the purple loose-strife, an alien plant, muskrats and other creatures' habitats are being destroyed in the Montezuma Refuge and other marshy, moist, and swampy areas. Muskrats are members of the rat and mice family. The muskrat actually has the same skull of a mouse only bigger. It is the nations' leading fur animal and is trapped on a strictly regulated basis. In New York State, muskrats reproduce easily, having several litters a year - more where the summers are longer, with from one to eleven in a litter.

They need unpolluted water with abundant vegetation, and eat the roots, bulbs and young stems of cattails. They eat some freshwater clams and each other if they get overcrowded. Their houses or lodges - dome shaped piles of cattails and mud - are rarely in water over two feet deep. When muskrats live in streams they burrow back into the banks. When they move into small ponds and burrow into the banks, they weaken the walls that hold the water and may cause the wall to rupture. Their enemies besides starvation or disease are the fox, mink, stray dogs, the great horned owl and themselves .

Up Route 89 and to the east is Howland Island, another wetland with a series of ponds and islands on the northern side of the Barge Canal. Howland's 400 acres were purchased in 1823 in soldiers script, awarded to Revolutionary War Veterans of the NYS Regiments. It was a farm until the late

1920's and New York bought it in 1932. The New York Department of Conservation manages it now as a refuge and it is a possible tract for exchange in the Native American Land Claim. It also offers a short canoe trip where you can feel you are deep in a wild swamp.

* * *

It appears on the map that Route 89 goes right to the shores of Lake Ontario but I find out it ends in the town of Wolcott in a "T". There are several roads through Wolcott but which one should I take?

I turn left looking for Route 89 and almost ended at Chimney Bluffs on Ontario Lake, an undeveloped state park. The unique land forms cut by the wind and rain are interesting, but Fair Haven State Park has a camping area and is further east. Relying on my sense of direction and not being afraid to ask directions, I zigzagged east on country roads surrounded by apple orchards toward Fair Haven.

Ontario's shore is not a smooth curve as the maps might lead you to believe. It has hundreds of assorted bays and marshes that extend far back inland, making it necessary to take the circle route to get to the next point of land. Although it is hilly, it is much less so than Ithaca. The flat expanses of water and marshes are a pleasant change.

After asking directions from a teenager licking an ice cream cone as he comes out of a drug store in Fair Haven, I am able to find the side entrance to the park. The front entrance is blocked off because they are blacktopping it. It is a long drive to the office near the new beach house with an oceanic view of the lake. The park's west boundary is a combination of cottages lining Little Sodus Bay and a boat launching ramp.

The eastern boundary is somewhere off in the distance. In the middle, the park surrounds a large pond called Sterling Pond. There is a narrow channel that connects the pond to the lake. The stream that feeds the pond is one of Mr. Erhling's canoe routes in his book Canoeing in Central New York. The narrow channel is the only place deep enough for diving and a life guard watches the swimmers there.

There are two long cement jetties that extend way out into the lake on either side of the large white sand beach. They are designed to keep the sand from washing away further down the shoreline, but when sand is kept from being moved by a jetty, it merely moves the problem elsewhere.

On the eastern side of the breakwater, beyond the swimming area, are huge Volkswagon-sized boulders that line the beach as rip-rap. Erosion has been a problem to the people living along the lake, partly due to the natural cycle of erosion to wash the shore back and partly because people think they can build right up to the water's edge and never have it change. It's easy to see why people like to live along the lake shore, but most of them are not aware of the water's seasonal cycles of buildup, tear down, create and destroy.

This Point has Native American Spirits too. It was used by the Seneca and Cayuga Native Americans for trading. They called it Little Seodose, hence the name Little Sodus Bay. There are eight-hundred acres here but it seems like more because the lake shore to the east is not developed for as far as the eye can see - yet.

I'm glad I brought the bike. There are not many sites open and the one I am able to get is as far from the entrance as possible. This camping section is on a slight hill overlooking the pond and it is probably the highest point in the park. The only reason I am able to get a place with out a reservation is because it is mid-week. It looks like a lot of people spend the whole summer here. With a small camper, it probably costs less to vacation here than to own a place on the shore, and you don't have the upkeep and taxes that way.

I am pleased with the site until I realize that it is on the path to the comfort station and right next to the water faucet which means more traffic, but it is convenient for me.

Changing into the bathing suit is done in record time and the only thing I unpack is the bike. It is all downhill to the white sand and wide expanse of blue sky over inviting water. There are sidewalks on either side of the main road and next to the pond. The pond looks shallow and is full of all kinds of water plants and little creatures.

I saunter into the lake and find that it isn't as warm as I thought it would be...It turns out to be a long wade. The sandy bottom slopes very gradually and I am far out into the lake before the water is up to my waist.

The sun is low and a cooling wind is coming off the water. Now I understand why there aren't many people in the water. In place of people, the beach is covered with sea gulls, hundreds of gulls. They are so crowded on the orange tiled roof of the bath houses that they make the roof look grey. On the beach the gulls strut in circles on claimed territory around the spread bath towels looking for tidbits to eat. They stay about six feet away from people but flock together quickly in groups of three or four if they think that one gull has found something good to eat.

It is relaxing to sit on the warm white sand and watch the gentle waves and distant boats making their way to far off places. That is until a four year old starts running all over the beach chasing the gulls and yelling, "Get out of here. Get out of here," at the top of his lungs. The reluctant gulls flap their wings two or three times, move out of the way and then the boy charges the next nearest group of gulls. The gulls have staked out imaginary territories and are arranged evenly over the entire beach. They are barely disturbed by the boy and seem to take the harassment as part of the job.

The gulls have adapted to man and thrive on garbage dumps, insect infested golf courses, grubs turned over by farmers' plows and sea food. They have nests on the islands in the lake and along the Saint Lawrence Seaway. After about 20 minutes of "get out of here", I decide to leave.

Scouting the roadside on the way back to the camp reveals that I'm not going to find any large pieces of firewood. There is plenty of small tinder because campers have switched to the easy light method, charcoal lighter fluid. Now I wish I had bought some charcoal while I was at the store. By the time I peddle back up the hill, I am comfortably warm again.

As I am trying to decide what to do for dinner, the park wood truck drives slowly around the circle. Generally there is an enterprising person that gets permission to sell wood to the campers, and I lucked out. The bundles of wood, according to the driver, weigh about sixty pounds and only cost two dollars and fifty cents. He assures me it's good wood, but one bundle, much more than a bushel basket full, is more than I want to spend, so I ask for a dollar's worth.

I think the fellow feels sorry for me. After I give him four quarters that I dig out of my pocket, he is generous and gives me about thirty pounds of wood.

The bailing twine cuts into my hand so much that I have to stop and bunch my handkerchief around the string before I can carry the wood the short distance back to the fireplace. I said I would carry it, even though he offered, it was a mistake. The second time I pretend to fix the handkerchief while I rest, by the fourth time I am close enough to the fireplace to half swing and half drop the wood. I should have paid attention - dry old wood doesn't weigh this much.

I feel I am being watched as I set up camp. I clear a place as far away from the path as I can so no one will trip over the tent lines in the dark and surprise both of us. There are a couple of trees and shrubs to tie the tent ropes to because the ground is hard here too. It is nice to be able to do things slowly, deliberately and carefully, including the job of splitting some of the wood into smaller pieces to burn long enough to start the larger ones.

It would be easier if I had had the hatchet but I'll use my all-in-one hip-denter's largest blade like a wedge and pound gently to drive it downward to separate the wood with the grain. I don't want to tempt breaking the knife, but I need several small pieces of wood.

It would not be an emergency here in the middle of a camp ground, but a broken knife could be disastrous in the wilderness. Nor did I want the knife to slip, hit the blade on the stone-bed of the fireplace or worse yet, cut myself. Cuts burns and falls are much easier to avoid than to repair.

Once the fire is snapping and smoking it is questionable that the loudly advertised seasoned "good" wood is all that it is said to be. As evening approaches there is the usual lessening of loud noises except for the barking of dogs.

Two campsites away in a pop-up canvas camper are two well trimmed little poodles. They sit in the front vinyl window and bark at anything that passes by on the road. When lacking entertainment, they move to the back window and bark at children playing intensive games. The barking, (or rather, high pitched yapping) is continuous, as there is a large assortment of children playing on the trails connecting the campsites with the wash house.

As things quiet down more, the dogs yapping seems to get louder. Some of the children leave for dinner. As dinner chores are completed, strolling couples slowly meander around the park, providing the dogs with more to yip at.

Now it is possible to hear increasing comments from other people about the dogs. The comments get nastier as time goes on and the noise drones on. About the time I decide to pay the poodles a visit with a few choice words, a police car pulls up in front of my campsite and the officer asks if I have seen the people who own the dogs or know where they went.

"Haven't seen them for awhile but I overheard them say they were going for a ride."

"Have they been barking long", he asks walking toward the dogs who promptly increase the intensity of their barking.

"Only since they left about an hour or so ago," I said trying not to overestimate. It's comforting to know that it is possible to get a hold of a policeman if necessary.

He walked over to the dogs and told them to be quiet. They responded by yapping furiously. The officer retreated to his car and called out with relief, "I'll be back in a while."

Comments from neighboring campers became louder and more numerous and outspoken. Any attempt to quiet the dogs only succeeded in getting them to yip louder. Conversations between vacationers now has a common subject and the camp begins to take on a tenseness.

After enduring another fifteen minutes of the grating yapping, I stomp confidently over to the trailer and scold the little grey monsters for making so much noise and tell them to shut up. My bold attempt only succeeds in stirring them into a frenzy of racing back and forth from window to window barking and growling protectively. I feel sheepish but at least I've tried. The commotion causes the children to congregate in front of the trailer, which makes them bark all the more. The children leave when the police car pauses briefly to note the situation hasn't changed.

This is happening while I am trying to cook dinner. The bargain wood will not burn well; it must be green. The steak that I bought to treat myself for not being able to backpack won't sear and ends up being dry and tough. I dump some freeze dried soup greens, a dash of pepper and the package of noodles from a package of Raman soup in the pot, but I should have only put in half the noodles.

Trying to ignore the dogs I watch a young family on the other side of me. They have three or four children and a medium size camper. A child in the camper is told to open wide for some medicine, "There, that isn't so bad. Here you can have your lollipop back."

"Waaa."

"Now it's time to go to bed."

"Waaa. I wanta mushmallow"

" I wanta mushmallow, too!"

To another child, "Let me change your bandages before you cook marshmallows."

"Oww, that hurts."

"You'll just have to be more careful where you ride your trike and not run into the bushes. There, now roast one for your sister first."

Slam!

"I want one, I want one."

Father says, "Just a minute and I'll get you a stick. Now be careful. It'll catch fire. Watch out."

Camper door opens, "Here's yours."

"Waa. I don't like it burned."

Lanterns are being lit and campfires spark as new logs are added. The mosquitos are arriving and the dogs are still yapping. Doing dishes is barely a chore, the only thing to wash is the fry pan and the fork. The noodles were enough for two people. I wonder how the vegetable and noodle mix will taste for breakfast?

It's almost dark when the owners of the dogs arrive and the barking stops. After mushy greetings to the dogs by the family, the daughter is directed to feed them. Soon metal pans are roughly put down on the ground and the dogs are silent except for slurping and the scraping of dishes as they are pushed around the bare ground as they try to get every last little bit of food.

After what I figure is a reasonable time, I walk over to the father. "Your dogs barked while you were gone. Someone complained and the police were here."

"Our dogs barked? Why, we've left them alone before and they didn't bark."

"Well they did tonight, almost continuously. I thought you would like to know because it bothered some people."

"We've gone camping before and they never barked."

"Just thought you would like to know." As I walk away the police car arrives.

The man explains, they just took a little ride and the dogs couldn't have made that much noise. The policeman suggests that they take the dogs with them when they leave the campsite. The man agrees but is unconvinced that they were barking. No more is heard from the dogs.

The mosquitos come out in full force as it gets dark. Another application of spray on my neck and hat keeps them at a distance, while I have my last cup of coffee. Perhaps there are better smelling people around. Mosquitos are said to prefer men over women, unwashed over washed, perfumed over no smell and light clothing over dark.

Hope no one trips over the tent ropes during the night.

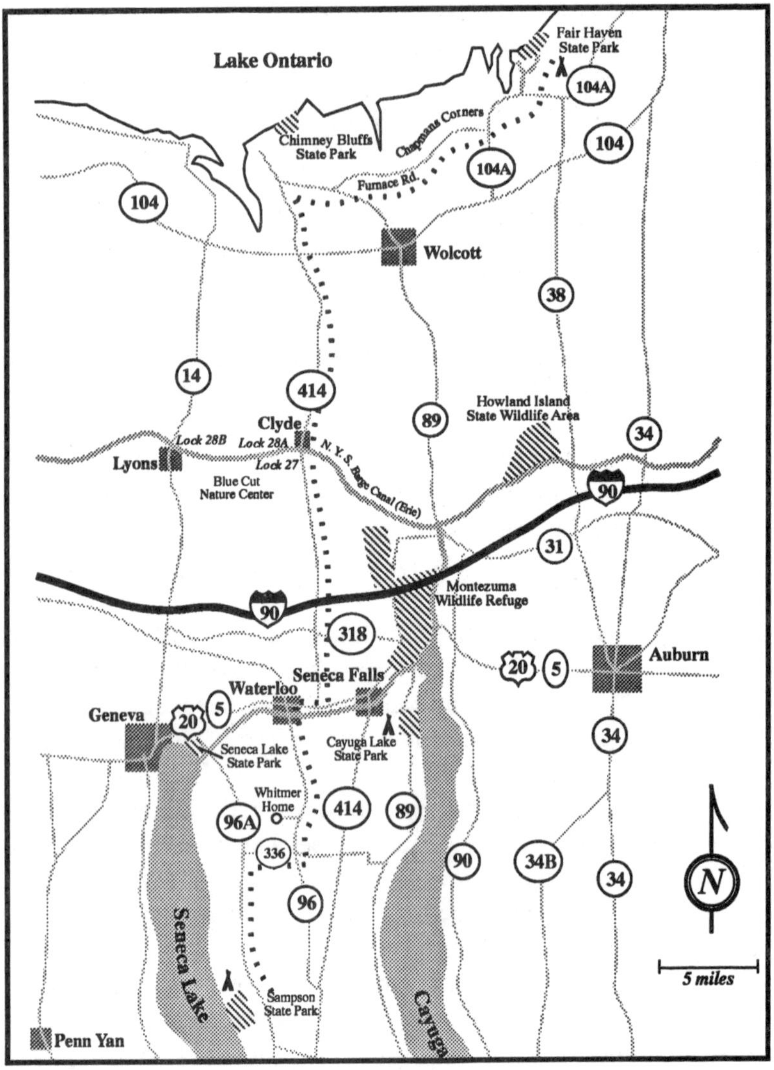

Hopscotch & Caravan

HOPSCOTCH & CARAVAN

When I look up at the heavens, the work of thy fingers, the moon and the stars set in their place by thee, what is man that thou shouldst remember him?
Psalm 8 vs 3 & 4

Up at six under an overcast sky. Have my usual breakfast over a smoky fire. Judging from the looks of other early risers, cooking breakfast over a fire isn't usually done.

Because it is early and it doesn't look like a lot of beach to explore, I only pack a snack, water and a rain jacket and change into hiking boots and long sleeve shirt.

I meet a couple of energetic people jogging in the early cool hours and a couple walking their dogs, but most of the early risers are preparing to go fishing on the lake. In fact, it looks like the fishing fleet is evacuating the bay. All kinds of boats are leaving, from small sail boats to snazzy inboards with several decks; antennas and fishing rods whipping as they make their way through far-spaced swells.

I have the park to myself as I bike across the bridge, along the beach road and through the empty parking lot to the far side of the park.

The weather looks uncertain; halfway between hazy and overcast. The lake is almost calm except for long swells that hardly disturb the water's surface; a far cry from the sea-like fury it is capable of.

I walk the bike as far as I can along the beach road and after checking to see that no one else is around, shove it into the bushes so it will not be so obvious. It looks like I will have the lake front all to myself.

Five foot wide boulders have been placed to form a wall at least fifteen feet wide at the base with about five feet showing above the water. All the flat sides have been angled to the beating waves. The tops are more or less flat and the wall is two or three boulders wide at the top. It is easy to make my way across the top, but it requires concentration to pick a route and not make a misstep on the rough rock or catch a toe in a crack.

All kinds of washed-up items are trapped between the rocks. Most of the debris is man-made and probably was tossed into the lake as garbage hoping it would sink. In order to look around at the endless horizon or between the rocks I have to stop long-stepping. I could spend all day checking each crack and cranny for treasure. Traveling down the long breakwall is like playing an endless game of hop-scotch. The breakwall must belong to the park because it is too massive to have been financed by a private person.

After about half a mile, the breakwall ends in a narrow pebble and shale beach. The width of the beach varies from almost nothing to twenty feet. In some places thick bushy shrubs grow over and dip their tips into the waves. In the far distance, hillside avalanches have toppled trees into the lake and carried them into the water, leaves first into the hungry waves.

A while ago people along the lake were protesting to town officials because the water was eroding their beach and destroying some of the cottages. Part of the protest was against the organization that controls the level of the lakes, part against the people who operate the canal and part against the politicians for not doing something. Ontario is around 245 feet above sea level. Trying to regulate the water levels ahead of predicted rain or droughts is nearly impossible. The amount of traffic on the Seaway as well as the generation of electricity affects the level somewhat. The lake isn't doing anything different than it has always done in its natural cycle of ups and downs. People shouldn't expect it to remain constant or build close to the water. They need to be reminded that nature is in a constant state of change.

Further down the beach, after squeezing between the water and some shrubs, I come upon a small pond not twenty feet from the lake's clawing waves. A blue heron "frahnk-frahnks" and flaps ponderously into the air as I push my way through the shrubs. An adult great blue heron may be four feet tall and have a wing span of six feet. The blue-grey bird wades along shore lines, in ponds and swamps looking for fish, frogs and crayfish. The heron has been known to seek mice, snakes and insects on land too. When it flies its neck is pulled in but the long legs trail out behind. Nesting normally occurs in colonies in isolated places such as the middle of swamps, islands on a lake and sometimes on land far from water. It has a small plume of feathers that lay over the head and stick out behind.

Because it is a wary bird, a great blue heron decoy is used to fool other birds into thinking it is a safe place to land. Wildlife photographers use the decoy when photographing water birds.

Watching the pond to see what other creatures are here, I can hear crows gossiping on the far side, sparrows flitting in the bushes and a woodpecker telegraphing a tree on the hillside. It must be a solar-lunar time.

There are certain times of the day that animals and fish tend to be more active besides the early morning and evening hours. Those times correlate with the solar-lunar tables, which show high and low tides as they pass across the earth. Animals (including us) are affected by the gravitational pull of the sun and moon. This means they will be more likely to be more active during the times of most and least pull, if there aren't other factors like a coming storm to affect them.

Little plops and waves in the water go ahead of me each time I take a step. The frightened frogs jump to safety as I step into their predetermined danger zone. A disturbed kingfisher rattles to the far side of the pond as unseen frightened ducks quack and splash into the air following the heron. The belted kingfisher is in a family all by itself in America. It is a blue-grey bird a little bigger than a robin with a large head, bushy crest and an over sized bill for catching fish. They fish by plunging into the water and then take the fish to a tree and swallow it whole. The king-

fisher is a solitary bird once the young are reared and can often be seen perched on a dead limb overhanging the water.

The kingfisher's nest is a chamber at the end of a three to six foot long burrow dug by the pair in a bank near water. They lay six or seven eggs on bare sand in the chamber.

The protected pond is a thick soup of water lily pads near the center, arrowhead plants along the edges of the brown water, and cattails merging the land with the water elsewhere. Stringy algae can be seen on the bottom of the pond where there aren't small green dots of duckweed covering the surface. Shrubs crowd to the edges where the land drops off into the deep water and behind the cattails.

The arrowhead tubers on the ends of long roots mature in the autumn. Once loosened they float to the surface for gathering. Arrowhead is a potato substitute and was the favorite food of the Lewis and Clark expedition. The arrowhead should not be confused with another plant, the pickerel-weed that looks similar but has closely clustered flowers on a spike like stalk and is a relative of skunk cabbage. Arrowhead has three petaled white flowers arranged in groups of three in a spiral on a long slender stem. Pickerel weed has purple flowers clustered around the stem.

The thickness of the surface plants control the temperature of the water beneath. Sometimes the duckweed is so thick it looks like a green carpet. The tiny duckweed plants are not attached to the bottom. It is the smallest flowering plant but rarely produces a flower, reproducing by breaking apart. There are twenty-five different species of duckweed which lack true leaves or stems. It is actually the stem that looks like a round leaf. It is the favorite food of many water birds.

Other people have visited this pond, but right now it is all mine to wonder at. It seems peaceful at first, but is actually strife torn with the war of survival of the fittest, eat or be eaten, grow in a space or be taken over. The battle is a silent one.

Purple loosestrife, an alien plant, has found its way here. It takes over marshes and offers nothing in return for crowding out the native plants that provide food and shelter for marsh and pond creatures. It is spreading fast and furiously all over New

York State and is impossible to get rid of except by pulling the whole plant out of the ground. Maybe someone will be able to find its weak point before it does more damage.

Most people do not recognize it as a pest because it has such pretty purple flowers on a long stalk, but the birds don't eat the seeds and nothing eats the plant. The only creature that is attracted to it is the nectar gathering ones like bees. It gives the honey a green cast which limits its use to baking.

* * *

A well weathered and wave-worn log provides a place for me to sit and explore the pebbles on the beach. Most of the beach pebbles have been worn to oval or triangular shapes. Years ago people came to the lake from many miles to collect the uniformly worn rocks to build the now famous cobblestone houses. Each stone is different from the others in some way although they have similar characteristics.

The large sail boats that left the harbor the same time I left have collected in a small circle not far out in front of me. They are having a coffee clutch or deciding their direction as the clouds are building tall, puffy towers and the sky is getting grey to the northeast.

It is still hazy to the west and wispy mares' tails are forming from moisture in the air. They indicate rain within twenty-four hours. The water is steel-grey under the northeastern grey clouds which seem to merge with the water. The water changes to light blue under the wispy clouds in the west.

The majority of the rocks and pebbles have a grey cast and look like shale, similar to those on Seneca Lake. By looking more closely, I am able to find a fossil of a plant that lived on the bottom of the ancient ocean.

There should be more driftwood here. It's fun to look for imaginary things in the twisted cast-up wood. Judging from the fire circles along the beach most of it must have been burned.

Wandering down the beach towards the eroded cliffs, I find a large dried-up dead carp, a relative of the gold fish, thrown up on the beach by some other day's storm waves, and a bright red balloon that some hopeful child released into the air with a long-since-gone postcard that would have said how far the balloon had sailed. There is a large assortment of plastic flotsam and jetsam that people hoped would sink and disappear, including disposable diapers, pieces of toys, fishing line, (death to any bird that gets tangled in it), plastic holders of six packs (a formidable hazard to wildlife) and an assortment of bottles and cans.

All along the shore, swamps finger their way inland between forested ridges that are being consumed slowly by the lake. In places there are bushels of long dead shriveled dried silvery alewives, sawbelly-like fish that are the lemmings of the lake and an important food source to some of the other fish. So far, they have not determined the reason for the seasonal die-off of the little fish.

Every so often I come across dark brown smelly snake-like eels curled as in their last minutes of fight for life. Mostly active at night, fresh caught smoked eels are a delicacy for some people. I wonder what killed these, perhaps they were spawning and died naturally.

I am not ready for the end of the walk nor ready to see the noisy people who appear on the stairs, heading down the trail.

* * *

The sky is becoming more ominous and the wind has become more than a breeze blowing from the north. The beach, water, air and vegetation are mine right now, I have it all to myself but the weather is in control. Progress along the beach now is slow because the clay cliffs are almost straight up and down; a wall into the water with a tangle of trees, roots and branches. It is a totally different environment than the pebbled beach or pond. It is hostile and every-thing seems to be clinging or hanging onto the barren clay cliff. The sky is threatening and the wind is blowing harder. The long swells have changed into swishing waves nibbling at the shore. There isn't any beach here: it's either clay or water. It's nearly impossible to climb through the tangled jungle and I can't see beyond the point to see how far the jungle of deadwood goes.

The waves are licking the bottom of the tree trunks along my route so I decide to turn around before the waves become so large that I'd have to walk in the unknown depth of water to get around the narrow places. I don't want to be in the position of having to get wet or confront the waves. If the weather didn't look like it would get worse I might go further, but past experience has taught me it is better to be safe than sorry. I decide to remain in control and head back slowly. I still haven't had any company, except for a fisherman in a small boat near the jetty at the edge of the sandy beach.

The walk back doesn't scare any more birds from the secluded little pond. It is as if everything has taken cover. Actually it is the middle of the day when most creatures rest. I haven't picked up my souvenir stone yet, it is a habit that I have had to limit because it can get too heavy.

The bike is still in the bushes when I get back and the first people I see are fishing along the lee side of the breakwater.

* * *

I heat the left over soup on the gas stove for lunch. When I pull the stove apart to pack it away, the valve in the can stays open and most of the gas comes out. I should have stuck the can back on the stem, but I just stand there stupidly and watch the misty cloud of gas spray out. Finally I wake up and shove the can back on the valve and try again, but I've lost most of the gas. It isn't a calamity because I bought the can on sale and have another full one tucked away.

I pack the gear, fold the dry tent, police the site and take a shower. The early afternoon is the best time to take a shower in a state park because there's lots of hot water, no waiting and no bugs.

Next time it would be fun to bring a canoe and explore Sterling Pond or other ponds. Fair Haven is not far from Sterling where they have an authentic reproduction of a Rennaisance village open weekends during the summer. The festival, put on by mostly college students, includes the clothes, food, entertainment and other activities of that time. They even have a dunking pond and stocks for people who misbehave.

Next stop Sampson State Park on the east side of Seneca Lake.

* * *

The Barge Canal, some of which is in the same place as the Old Erie Canal, was called Clinton's Ditch while it was being built. The forethought and perseverance of Dewitt Clinton to build the canal was one of the more important events in American history. Not only was it the engineering feat of the day, it helped to unify New York and provided a reasonably comfortable and inexpensive method of transportation west. It allowed the produce of rural New York to be transported to Albany and New York City and brought money back to the people.

The project was officially started July 4, 1817 and although it cost seven million dollars to build, it paid for itself in a few short years after it was officially opened from Lake Erie to Sandy Hook New Jersey in October 1825. Most of the labor was supplied by Irish immigrants and new stanzas were added to their work songs as they dug the canal. Part of a song sung while digging through Montezuma Swamp was:

We are digging the Ditch through the mire;
Through the mud and the slime and the mire, by heck!
And the mud is our principal hire;
In our pants, up our sleeves, down our neck, by heck!
The mud is our principal hire.

Part of the song E-R-I-E tells that it was not always an easy journey from one end of the Canal to another.

We were forty miles from Albany,
Forget it I never shall
What a terrible storm we had that night,
On the E-R-I-E Canal.
O-o-oh, the E-R-I-E was a-rising,
The gin was a-getting low,

And I scarcely think
We'll get a drink
Till we get to Buffalo-o
Till we get to Buffalo.

Low Bridge-Everybody Down and Fifteen Years on the Erie Canal were sung as the horses or mules pulled the barges along. There were bridges over the Canal that connected farms and towns. In many cases there was barely enough clearance for the barge much less a passenger sitting on the top deck. In fact some of the barges didn't allow anyone on the top deck to fall asleep for fear of being hit and knocked overboard by a low bridge.

Growth of cities depended upon where the canal came through. Although a railroad, built with excess funds from the canal income, took some of the freight and passenger business from the canal, it was continually widened from the original forty feet and deepened from the original four feet and in some places another system of locks was built for traffic going the other way. Shipping by water is still a reasonable way to ship. Because the Erie paid its way so well it remains a free waterway.

Along the towpath where mules once pulled the barges, there is a hiking trail linking Canal Parks in Monroe County to the Newark Canal Park. There are also trails along the Canal in Syracuse, and an interesting Erie Canal Museum.

Further past where 318 turns into 96 is Phelps, the Sauerkraut Capital of the World. While sauerkraut is one of the many famous New York products that is shipped all over the world, peppermint is probably a lesser-known Phelps product.

An old story has it that in 1833 a peddler found a peppermint plant growing wild nearby while selling his wares and remedies. At that time most of the peppermint for flavorings and medical purposes was imported from the East. He recognized the newfound plant as being as good as the imported plant from Japan and China. He meticulously collected it and bottled it in blue bottles. Although now it is grown out west, to my knowledge it is still processed and bottled in Phelps because of the quality reputation of their peppermint flavoring in the blue bottle.

Route 414 continues south towards the town of Waterloo and the Seneca River which connects Seneca Lake via the Cayuga Canal to the Barge Canal.

Waterloo is where Henry C. Welles had the idea of honoring our soldiers by decorating their graves on a May Day in 1866 beginning the Memorial Day Observance. Today, Waterloo has a Memorial Day Museum on Main Street, Routes 5 & 20.

History buffs will find much to inspire them in the Finger Lakes region including a museum of airplane history in the town of Hammondsport at the southern end of Keuka Lake. To the east of Waterloo is the town of Seneca Falls, home of the Woman's Hall of Fame and the Woman's Rights National Historic Park on Fall Street. The first Woman's Rights Convention was held here in 1848, and there is an annual festival in July complete with art, music and a reenactment of the original convention. Seneca Falls is also the birthplace of the Republican Party.

I turn west on 5 & 20 looking for a gas station. Route 5 used to be the main east-west stage coach and mail route. It cost 5 cents a mile to ride and allowed no more than fourteen pounds of baggage per person. In 1797 it took three days of body battering to get to Utica from Geneva, about one hundred miles. The Geneva Hotel, was one of the nicest of the time, and people often stayed over to rest for the next stage because the ride was so taxing.

It took one week to bounce and jounce to Buffalo from Albany. The spring, summer and fall traffic was not limited to stage coaches. There were drovers; people who herded the country produced cattle and poultry to the city markets. Besides having to pay the road tolls, the drovers paid for safe passage over Indian land with an animal of the Indian's choice. The Wells Fargo Company had its home port in the stage coach town of Auburn.

On the outskirts of Waterloo there is a rustic shopping complex. The stores are called Ye Olde Feed Bag, Ye Olde Country Store, Ye Olde Gift Store, Ye Olde Craft Store, and Ye Olde Saw Mill. Each is reminiscent of colonial times and craftsmanship. The restaurant, Ye Olde Feed Bag is a local coffee and doughnut place and has a full lunch menu with homemade bread, muffins, pies, and soups.

After getting gas and checking the oil, I turn south on 96. It is a country road almost exactly halfway between Seneca and Cayuga Lakes. To the south, it angles east and goes to Ithaca. There is very little except farms, a few houses and the edge of Seneca Army Depot on the road, so when I find myself behind a tour bus with "Jeans" written across the back I am puzzled.

Why would a big bus be taking a narrow secondary road out into the country when there are so many other nice highways to go on¿ It's going my way so I'll follow it and see.

We drove a few miles when I notice out of the corner of my eye, a sign that said Peter Whitmer Farm, Free Tours. I like animals and this must be a special dairy farm. There are a lot of dairy cows in the Finger Lakes. New York is one of the top dairy producers of cheese dry milk and milk products in the country. If the tour looks interesting, I might go too, if that is where the bus is going. When the bus signals to turn right, I signal to turn right, following along behind the big "Jeans" bus, wherever it is going.

We drive along for a mile or so on a narrowing road and the bus stops. I stop. I am right behind the bus and can't see why it has stopped.

We sit for a while, and because the road has narrowed I wonder if the "Jeans" bus might not know where it is going. A minute passes and the driver's arm sticks out the window and waves me on. Now what¿...There is a stop sign at the intersection but that doesn't explain why the bus didn't go on or turn. The road changes to gravel up on the rise and I hope that the farm is up ahead or there is a place to turn around.

What if the bus is waiting to follow me¿ This is what I get for following a bus. I fumble for the map I put away because I knew where I was going when I started out,...before I decided to caravan with the bus.

Over the slight rise, the road narrows still more into a lane and seems to disappear in the distance. I'll have to find a place to turn the cumbersome van around very soon.

My stomach is getting that sinking feeling. As I pass a tall hedgerow, I see a large vacant parking lot and a striking white co-

Jeans

lonial building. It looks like a chapel with two small identical buildings on either side. The new looking building is attractive, so after once around the parking lot I decide to investigate and park the van. The bus pulls in, parks in front of the building and the people file out.

Most of the people are dressed nicely and here I am with walking shorts: at least I have a clean blouse on. The group is a mixture of ages from teenage to retirement, but none look as sporting as I do.

As they file through the heavy double door into the building, I step in line behind and join them. At the door we receive an official welcome to the Peter Whitmer Farm by a man in a Sunday-go-to-meeting suit and are told that the film will be ready in a minute and we can wait in the chapel.

Now what have I gotten into?

The building is cool. The room we are led into is a church! The chapel is white inside and without ornamentation or pictures. Wood moldings are applied in straight and curved lines and are the only decorations on the ceiling and walls. The ceiling is at least 25 feet high. Red carpeting and cushions on white church benches make it simple but impressive. There is a movie screen on the side wall at the back of the chapel. The thirty people from the bus and I sit on folding chairs with best church manners. Obviously, the group knows I don't belong with them and I think the guide noticed too; I stick out like a sore thumb.

Too late to leave the cool chapel now, so I wait wondering what is going to happen next, and study the impressive church. Soon the lights dim and the movie tells us that this is the farm where Joseph Smith, the first President of the Church of Jesus Christ of Later-Day Saints and six witnesses formally signed the papers to organize the church, known to some as the Mormons. The name comes from Moroni's father, Mormon, who was the major compiler of the ancient records. This happened on the farm on April 6, 1830. Joseph Smith's home is in Palmyra, New York, about 25 miles from here. It is where the famed outdoor free spectacle of the Hill Cumorah Pageant is held every year each evening the last week of July.

According to the movie, Joseph, 14 years old, felt it was time to join a church. All the local churches were putting on membership drives and he sought an answer to which one to join by praying in the woods nearby. Two people of heavenly origin appeared to him and told him not to join any of the churches and they would reveal more as time went on. Seven years and several visits later, he was told about the ancient golden records hidden in a hill, Hill Cumorah, that he would translate.

The golden plates were from a great civilization that inhabited the Americas from 600 BC to 420 AD and told the history of that civilization and about a visit of Jesus Christ to them.

This radical claim put Joseph in an unpleasant situation and soon many people were against him and his followers. The golden records disappeared, as it was said they would after they were translated into the Book of Mormon. The Book of Mormon was supposed to be a supplement to the Bible we know. Because Joseph's ideas were considered blasphemy, he and his followers were driven out of town and after much persecution, established their headquarters in Salt Lake City, Utah.

Although their basic ideas did not conflict with the existing Christian religions, they allowed polygamy which aroused much anger against the group. The Mormons believe in actively pursuing the career one is best suited for and getting an education for it. They believe in devoting a part of their lives to the betterment of all through church and community activities.

They believe in the day of rest and religious contemplation and one day a week is set aside for activities as a family. They abstain from anything that abuses the body: like smoking, or the mind, like gambling.

As our tour group is ushered out the side door, I find out that the "farm" is a simple log cabin, located in a reproduction of a garden of the 1830's. The open hearth cabin has been restored to look like it might have in 1830. I find out that the group that I've joined has traveled from Florida as pilgrims to visit the historical sites of their religion. One of the pleasant people even invited me to contact someone locally for continued study of their beliefs and to visit the Hill Cumorah Pageant.

Over twenty-five people, not including the huge chorus and people backstage, perform on 25 hillside stages on seven nights. It is a moving story presented to thousands and as far as I know it has never rained on one performance yet.

This has been an unexpected stop on my retreat and has added new thoughts to ponder.

* * *

Where 96 intersects with 336, I turn east, along the northern border of the Seneca Army Depot toward Seneca Lake and Route 96A, home of the famous white deer.

Scientists have been unable to determine the reasons for the many white deer on Depot grounds. There are no predators (except dogs) and the deer population has on occasion grown to the point of eating itself out of food. Controlled archery hunts have been allowed during the season to hunters with special permits.

The white deer are not albinos but have all or partial white coats. The white coloring makes it easier to see them as you ride along the Depot boundaries. There has been much speculation about whether it is heredity, environmental forces or both causing the unnatural mutated white deer.

Routes 96 and 96A run along either side of the Depot in the town of Romulus. I expected to go past the farm where the Woman's encampment is but it must be on another road. Set back from the road are wire fences strung with barbed wire. The grass is mowed on either side of the fence and on the far side of a road that is parallel to the fence.

The fence brings fleeting memory of the recently fallen Iron Curtain. In Germany there were sentry boxes every 1,000 yards, floodlights, double coils of barbed wire behind a high fence, dogs on patrol on a parallel road and in between and a wide raked area to show footprints. All to keep a captive people in. Here the fence is to keep people and women from protesting nuclear missile deployment of fantastically destructive war "deterrents" from the not-officially-admitted nuclear storage area. For those of us that live free and relatively untroubled, well fed lives, the monster caged in our "backyard" is thought about with as much enthusiasm as the closet monsters of childhood nightmares. Forgotten, it disappears and doesn't nag one's responsibilities towards world peace.

The Seneca Army Depot is not the only military installation to have been here. Down the road on the shore of Seneca Lake are the remnants of a Naval training station that covered 2,500 acres and had 208 buildings housing 60,000 men. Some of it was used by the Air Force for the Korean War. No longer needed, it was closed in 1956, and in 1960 part of it was re-opened as Sampson State Park.

* * *

New York State promised each of its Revolutionary Soldiers 600 acres of land for their services. Much of the land north and between Seneca and Cayuga Lakes was included in the 1,500,000 acres set aside. Of course not all of the land was claimed. There were squatters and some mismanagement which led to all kinds of disputes and title searches, not to mention that the land was "assumed" from the Indians. The soldiers from Sullivan's Expedition were impressed by the beauty of the land and many came back here to settle.

Here was a vast land with wildlife resources just waiting to be taken, to be conquered. Asheries were established to make lye and potash from the ashes of the trees cut to clear the land. The trees and wildlife were part of the wealth and once cleared, the marginal land between the lakes was soon "used up". Once mined of its riches many of the people deserted and became pioneers traveling by wagon train to the "rich" lands of the west. However, people who are world travelers say that this area is far superior to all others they have visited. It wasn't very long ago the Seneca Indians roamed here, and the controversial Cayuga Indian Land Claim dispute is still unsettled at this time. A previous ruling by the Supreme Court in favor of the Oneida Indian Claim to 100,000 acres in Madison County may help the Cayuga prove that 64,015 acres "bought" under a 99 year lease from the Seneca in 1795 and 1807 was illegal.

Sampson State Park has 245 campsites with electric hookups in five loops of open, gently sloping lawn. There are a few scattered trees, but most of the sites are out in the open. The majority of the trees are in the small gullies that drain into the lake and along the steep bank of the lake. At one time, the Finger Lakes State Parks and Recreation Commission thought of naming Sampson "Kendaia State Park" for the original Seneca name known as Appletown for the apple orchards the Indians had here. The burial grounds for the Indian Village Ken-Dai-A is on the Seneca Army Depot grounds, not far away.

With the help of the Ranger in the Park Office I picked a site in the middle loop on the map that he said was between two tall cottonwood trees.

There are only about five other people camping in this loop that will accommodate 40 tents or RVs. The lake is hidden by the trees along the bank about 500 yards away. The tops of the distant smoke stacks of the electrical generating plant in Dresden on the opposite shore can be seen above the trees. It is a coal fired steam plant that uses the water from the lake to cool the steam back into water to reheat again. The heated water is discharged back near the end of Keuka Outlet and the year long warm water makes the right conditions for some fish. The by-product of the plant is fly ash which has to be trucked away after it has settled out in one of several ponds around the plant. As yet no safe use has been found for the tons of powdery ash produced and so it is buried near-by on farm land near the Outlet.

It is hot, muggy and overcast since the grey clouds have moved in during the early afternoon. Of course there is no wood nearby to scrounge, so I'll have to make due with the three pieces left over from this morning, unless I can pick up some driftwood from the lake. It should be plentiful because the prevailing wind is toward this side of the lake.

I pitch the tent so I will have the morning sun in the window and the afternoon shade from the trees. The ground is baked clay and another peg breaks when it hit a root. That makes three broken. When I try to tie one of the tent ropes onto a thick piece of jagged bark on the tree, I notice a vine growing up the trunk! Poison ivy!

As long as the wind doesn't blow hard, the tent should stay up. In case it decides to rain I won't put the mattress in the tent yet. Now for a swim and to explore the lake front. Two pumps on the bike and a long gliding ride puts me at the swimming area, which is diagonal to the campsite.

As I arrive the life guards are packing up because no one is swimming, a good excuse for me to take just a quick swim. No wonder! With the cool grey choppy water and the cool wind it doesn't take long to get cold.

Right out in front in the middle of the lake is a large grey barge with a large crane. It is a Navy installation that is anchored there year round. Their access dock is located in Dresden on the opposite shore. At night it is lit up like a construction project with yellow sodium vapor lights.

Small boats go back and forth to it almost continuously. The double barge is a floating laboratory used for testing sonar, which is underwater radar. Sonar is used to locate objects and ships in the water. The Navy picked Seneca Lake because it is large and deep, resembles the oceans with layers of different temperatures of water, and is much less vicious than the ocean weather wise.

Now that I am chilled, I can get warm by peddling up the hill, but not until I check the beach for wood. There is lots of driftwood but it's been burned at beach fires. No campfire can beat one on a beach. There is something about the combination of fire and water... Looking forward to a warm meal I scatter cooking equipment on the table. While splitting one of the three pieces of wood for a fire, a shiny new Blazer drives in with a large, super fancy inboard motorboat and backs into a space diagonally across from mine.

Sampson is where they have had the Annual Thunder on the Lake races of the super fast Hydroplane boats. The noise of the engines can be heard echoing around the lake when they are racing. This boat is large enough to camp in and is not one of the hydroplanes that they put into the lake with a crane. Next a new van drives in pulling a forty foot camping trailer and parks next to the boat. After they block the trailer up, they take the boat down to the marina to launch it.

The smoky fire finally boils the water for a one pan dinner of macaroni and cheese. There wasn't enough cheese flavor to suit me so I break up a slice of cheese, add some butter buds (freeze dried butter without the fat) dry milk and Italian seasonings. Mmm, good and also hot. After a cup of coffee, I boil more water and make a thermos of tea, and eat a strawberry roll-up for dessert. As I finish cleaning up and think about exploring, it starts to rain lightly. I move my towel from the bike basket to a clothes hook in the van, make a trip to the comfort station, located in the center of the loop and retire to read about the adventures of Sacakagaweha.

* * *

It pounds thunder, flashes lightning and pours hard several times during the night.

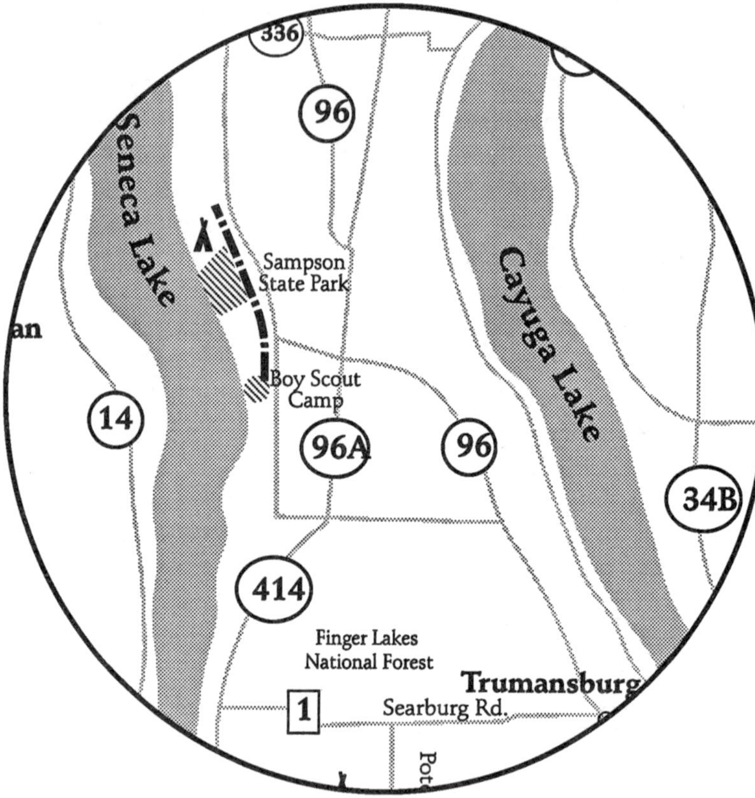

Storm Clouds & Boy Scouts

STORM CLOUDS & BOY SCOUTS

The heavens tell out the glory of God, vault of heaven reveals his handiwork. One day speaks to an other, night with night shares its knowledge, and this without speech, or language or sound of any voice. The music goes out through all the earth, their words reach to the end of the world.

Psalms 19 vs 1-4

It's still raining when I wake up before seven. The rain soaked the ground enough for the wind to loosen the partially driven stake that held up the front pole. When it leaned over, it let the rain in and there is a nice puddle in the middle of the tent floor. I fix the pole so it won't get worse. I hope the old wives tale of rain before seven quit before eleven will apply today. I'll read a while.

Eventually, I give up waiting for the rain to stop and venture out in a rain jacket in mid-morning to make some brunch. A wood fire is out of the question - no wood. So I get out the aluminium foil bowl I packed with dry cereal, sprinkle some dry milk on it, add some raisins, a little water and a squeeze of honey and eat breakfast. The plastic bag I put on the bench to keep my seat dry blows off as I try to light the little gas stove to heat water. I don't want a completely cold breakfast on such a dreary cool day. The wind keeps blowing the match out, so after I finish the cereal I make a wind break with the aluminium foil and finally get the water heating. When I sit down on the bench I find out that the plastic has blown away. As I struggle with breakfast, the hood of my rain jacket keeps pushing hair into my eyes, or the wind blows it off completely. The wind is trying to blow everything it can off the table. The people in the fancy camper are

having bacon, eggs, toast and hot coffee listening to the news and watching me, at least in my imagination.

Several foil chases later I realize that it has stopped raining. The picnic table is under the trees and it's the wind shaking the water off the leaves that is making the sound of rain, but it looks like it could start again anytime.

At least clean-up won't take very long. I hope it gets warmer because the wet seat isn't very comfortable. Now what? I'll straighten up the van and see if the sky improves.

Not much change, so I change into dry shorts and read a little more. I tire of that quickly and since I have mastered the trick of lighting the stove in the wind, I get up and make a pot of popcorn. Sitting around will never do. Back into my jeans and rain coat, I'll pack a snack and, hike along the lake front to the south. Above the marina is a concession stand where I splurge on a hot cup of coffee and an order of hot, salty french fries to get fueled up for the hike.

The marina has spaces for 126 boats and about half are filled. There are four young people launching a Hobie Cat, a two hulled boat called a catamaran. Although some of them look like they know what they are doing, the one elected to sail it into the slip is having an awful time making it go where he wants. The gusty wind is from the north and the boat doesn't want to turn, even though he has the center board down. It keeps getting "in irons" (when the boat stalls, won't move at all or goes backwards).

The weather looks promising to the south but dark clouds are coming from the north. Ready for some exercise, I walk south along the water's edge. The beach is made up of all sizes and shapes of stones. They are round and looser near the water's edge and walking on them is like walking on a sandy beach; you always slip a little. The waves have deposited the stones or moved them according to their weight and the power of the waves. The beach is a series of strips of similar stones one to two feet wide back to the shrubs on the bank.

The stones are packed more firmly about six feet back from water. In the winter, when the water is low, many of the smaller stones are washed out leaving baseball size and larger stones exposed. The small fine gravel is replaced in the spring by the high water. Shrubs and poison ivy have crept onto the summer beach in many places. In order to walk a reasonably straight line and avoid poison ivy, I choose the harder walking, close to the water.

Out into the ruffled water about a foot, the bottom is firm again but I don't want to get my leather boots wet. A nice warm day and sneakers would work, but no way am I going to go barefoot. There are pieces of broken colored glass, mostly worn smooth by the wave action, and bits and pieces of pretty pink clam shells that are not worn down and have ragged, sharp edges.

The former owners of the shells, members of the paper shell family, spend part of their lives as parasites. The parent clam carries the embryos for almost a year until they are ejected. They are only one-fiftieth of an inch long and snap at any disturbance in the water. This, if they are lucky, helps them latch onto a passing gill or fin of a fish. The fish obliges by growing a protective cover over the invader. After two or three weeks the clam has developed enough to go out on its own and drops to the bottom.

Clams are at the lower end of the food chain and are fortunate if they survive bottom feeding fish and crayfish. If they grow larger they become food for raccoons, mink, turtles and birds. Although they have pink to white pearly interiors, they are not the clams used for buttons. Lucky paper shell clams may grow up to be six inches wide.

Past experience attempting to cook them from Seneca Lake, (cooked because they have parasites too), resulted in a rubbery tasteless blob (in the Adirondacks they were more palatable.) If you have to eat them, try chopping them up in a chowder or some other soup where you wouldn't have to chew them much.

There are other kinds of clams in the Finger Lakes and ponds but these are the ones whose pink shells you see washed up on the shore. We've tried putting a couple of live clams in our goldfish tank but they didn't last long. I think there wasn't enough food in the water and there might not have been enough current for them to sieve out their food. Because we had a filter in the water, much of their food was taken away and I'm sure there was other microscopic life that was missing too. Clams filter the water to get their food and if the water is polluted it is possible for them to collect enough poison and die. A good reason to make sure the water is clean if you are going to eat clams. By poisoning one source of food in a food chain it is sure to have an effect on the other animals in the chain.

Another parasite in the lake is the sea lamprey. This not a native to the lake but has come up from the ocean through the Barge Canal. There is a control program in progress on Seneca Lake and it seems to be working well.

An adult lamprey eel searches out a gravel bed in a feeder stream and lays its eggs. When the eggs hatch, the larva burrow into a muddy bottom further downstream. There they eat algae and plant material for up to eleven years. Then something triggers them to develop their round mouth full of saw-like teeth for rasping a circle into a fish. They swim down stream into the lake where rainbow trout, lake trout, brown trout, perch and pike are waiting for food to be washed down to them. Instead they become food for the sawing teeth of the lamprey.

The lamprey attaches itself and digests the fishes' flesh, sucking juices and blood. If the host fish is large enough it might survive, but usually the lamprey out-grows its host or the host dies and the lamprey has to search for a new dinner.

There has been a very carefully conducted series of treatments on the water to kill the larva in the muddy streams and silty delta areas in Seneca Lake. The Department of Environmental Conservation was fortunate to have had all the conditions in their favor when they treated and as much as 80% of the larva were killed near and in Keuka Outlet. However as the lampreys in the lake mature, they will come up stream and lay eggs and the cycle will start all over again, so the result of this treatment will not be known for a while.

There are two kinds of treatment, one for the lake, which consists of dropping granules that will sink to the bottom where the larva are, and a liquid which is used in the stream.

In spite of controls and non-toxicity to other creatures, people on Cayuga Lake, where they also have a lamprey problem, have protested the use of the chemicals. One of the chemicals used is similar to that given to mammals for tape worms. The chemicals have been used for a number of years in the control of lampreys in the Great Lakes by the federal government. The people were able to delay the treatment in Cayuga for the moment, making Cayuga a way of comparing success.

The result so far: Seneca fisherman are getting fewer fish with the ugly lamprey scars on them, less fish with the lampreys still attached and the fishing is improving.

Seneca and Cayuga Lakes rely on stocking of the trout by the DEC because breeding habitat on the bottom of both lakes has been destroyed by the erosion of soil into the lake from farms and construction. The silt has covered the gravel beds which the trout need for eggs to develop. Keuka is the only Finger Lake that still has some gravel beds suitable for reproduction.

The further I walk from the marina the more driftwood I find, but there isn't much of the artistic twisted kind. Because there are few signs of previous visitors, I imagine I am combing the beach as it might have been hundreds of years ago. Detouring around shrubs that have grown down to the water puts me further back in time. As the beach becomes more wild, so does the bank. On a small point are the ruins of an old building, probably a sentry shack, overgrown with brambles and littered with branches and downed trees. There is a tipped over crumbling cement patio and breakwall being claimed by the lake. With grape vines and shrubs growing into the door, it wouldn't be surprising to see a sleek cat stalking, a large snake slithering, or colorful birds darting among the dark shadows of the tropical setting.

It is possible that these grape vines are escapees from a nearby vineyard, or perhaps the great grandfather, of the vines in the vineyard. The majority of the grapes that are grown here in the Finger Lakes were developed from hearty native grapes. The blue-purple Concord and White Niagara are used in wine, juice and as a table grape. Demand by wine makers encouraged growing varieties of wines from Europe to compete with European wines, but they are not as hardy or disease resistant and need more care.

According to wine makers, the public is drinking more white wine than red now and so the poor farmer that has acres of Concords is getting less and less money per ton, if he can sell them at all. But since red wine has been found to help reduce chloresterol, demand for the Concord should increase.

Since New York passed a home winery law that allows a farmer to make his own wine, many of them are turning to home wineries to survive; others are just going out of business.

The sunny slopes, poor rocky soil, and weather mellowed by the lakes, makes much of the land around the lakes productive vineyards, where they could not be tilled for regular crops because of erosion. Even so, erosion is a serious problem here.

A vineyard needs lots of care to produce the triangular bunches of grapes that make the royal juice. During the winter or in early spring the vines must be pruned. The trained craftsmen that brave the snows and cold winds don't last long if they don't enjoy being outside.

The cuttings must be gathered from between the rows. Some are kept to root to replace old vines. Of late a new craft of making vine wreaths has made use of some of the prunings. Well cared-for vines may produce for twenty-five years and more.

Before the buds swell and after the vines have thawed, they must be tied to wires to give the vines support, to keep them from blowing over in the winds of summer thunder storms, and to allow the maximum sunlight on most of the leaves.

They are sprayed for wilt, mold diseases and insects that might attack them and hopefully there will not be a late freeze when they flower. There is no protection against the mice in the winter, except to keep grasses and other plants from growing around the vines and between the rows. The mice girdle the vines by eating the cambium layer protected under the snow. Nor is there anything to keep the deer from eating the tender new shoots or the grapes in the fall. Once the vines are growing vigorously they must be suckered. The new growth around the bottom of the main vine must be cut off or it will sap the strength away from grape development.

When the grapes are ripe they are picked either by hand or machine. Hand picking is tedious but occurs during the unmatched beauty of Fall's warm days and cool nights. Machine picking, a relatively new development, shakes the grapes off the vine with a high tractor-like shaker that straddles the wire. Hand picking gets the grapes on steep hillsides and those left at the end of the rows if the vineyards haven't been arranged for the machine. The problem with machine picking is it shakes loose everything: ripe grapes, poor grapes, leaves, insects, and even an occasional bird's nest now occupied by a mouse family taking advantage of a live-in dining room.

The Finger Lakes region has about 89 wineries with at least 20 of them around Seneca and Cayuga Lakes. Many of them have tours and tastings. Many believe the wine and juice produced here are far superior to other areas. Mavco of Elmira has an interesting color map of the wineries and other points of interest around Seneca Lake.

The preserving of foods, especially grapes in the form of wine-making, has a long and interesting history. Sap from grape stems provides a cool drink in the summer, but it will harm the plant to cut it. The best grapes are in the vineyard. Wild grapes are more persistent and resistant to damage and disease, and provide food for birds. Farmers have a gas cannon that makes a loud bang, at intervals to try to scare the birds away from the ripening grapes. After a while the birds, particularly robins, learn to ignore the sudden noise, so the cannon is moved to another spot. Farmers also have to contend with deer, raccoons, fox, turkey, opossums and squirrels eating their grapes. For awhile the noise was a source of anxiety to some of the returned Vietnam Vets.

Grape leaves and young shoots are also edible in a pinch, if they haven't been sprayed, but the roots of the grape vine are poisonous. There are Middle East recipes that call for grape leaves in some of the exotic tasty foods. Our local annual County Fair always has some patient church ladies who bake grape pie for the refreshment booths. Recent pink grape juice has been developed to provide another outlet for some of the older varieties of grapes and has been so well received that markets haven't been able to keep it in stock.

I keep looking back over my shoulder to keep an eye on the dark rolling clouds. Actually I like the rain; its being out in the lightning I don't like. The wind has picked up and the black clouds are getting taller and tumbling violently over one another.

When the thunder starts it is not surprising, but after it continues for so long I realize it is a jet cargo plane coming in for a landing at the Depot. It creates an immense vibration of the air as it comes lower and lower, reminding me of the irony of nature's beauty and man's determination to make war.

When I reach a small wooden dock with boats pulled up on the beach next to it, I want to go further, but don't know how populated the shore is or exactly where the steep cliffs are, so I turn back. Still it would be fun to walk all the way around the lake.

The thick black clouds are dropping a veil of rain as they creep down the lake. Now flashes of lightning fork to the hillsides and occasionally to the water. Let's see who gets to the marina first, me or the rain.

The challenge of getting back before the rain doesn't allow me time to search for the usual memento stone. Great big drops of rain begin to splat the windshield just as I unlock the van door. Next stop-Babcock Hovey, a Boy Scout Camp about five miles down the lake on the other side of Willard. Willard is known for Willard State Hospital, first established as an agricultural college, in 1869 it became the Willard Asylum for the Insane, then changed to Willard State Hospital. Now it has a large out-patient service for alcohol rehabilitation. Its nearness to the Boy Scout Camp makes it a source of tall tales that keep some Scouts anxious about night visitors.

Cayuga and Seneca are only nine miles apart here. Less than two miles to the east is the town of Ovid. Organized in 1794, Ovid is one of the oldest towns in the area. The municipal park, Sheldrake, is located on Cayuga Lake. Ovid is known for its "Three Bears", identical municipal buildings built next to one another but one third the size of the one next to it.

To the north, not far from the Whitmer Farm, is the town of Varick where balloonists and sky divers enjoy their sport. Also in the Township of Varick is the Rose Hill Mansion. Built with

Greek Revival lines, it is open to the public for tours.

Five miles south of Willard is the Town of Lodi and Lodi Point State Park where you can see Silver Thread Falls, which is higher than Niagara Falls. Lodi Center, south of the village of Lodi is near the northern end of the Interloken Trail and Mill Creek Stream which feeds Lodi Point Park.

Exploring the fall-washed Finger Lakes gullies is great fun, but you must pick the best time of the year for water flow and never go by yourself. Be prepared with good boots and clothing. A short stream on a map has a way of meandering all over as well as presenting cliffs, gorges and dead tree dams. It is also important to get permission from the land owners, some of whom might enjoy the excuse to accompany you because few farmers have the time for that kind of pleasurable outing.

The scenic beauty of the Finger Lakes takes on a new dimension with winter snows. There are more than two dozen places for down-hill or cross country skiing, not to mention the trails and county parks available.

Bicycling the Finger Lakes is one way to see more without vehicles and improve your physical fitness. There are clubs and events in Auburn, Ithaca, Rochester, Syracuse and Binghamton. One group out of Rochester offers a variety of tours. There is a book of 20 Bike Tours you can get from your library and the Finger Lakes Guide has information on bike tours, group tours and other excursions.

* * *

I had an invitation to attend the weekly campfire presentation of skits and advancement at Babcock Hovey from my Scoutmaster husband and two scout sons. My planned early arrival at the Scout Camp meant an invitation to the weekly hot dog roast prepared by all the Scoutmasters. What luck, the storm moved diagonally to the west without any more rain. So the welcome dry cookout included slightly burned hot dogs and an update on the antics and accomplishments of the troop during the week.

Before dark, parents and members of the Scout's families congregate at an outdoor platform in a hayfield for a huge bonfire, songs, skits and summaries of each troop's merit badges and special awards. After the entertainment, parents, staff and Scout Masters are invited to the dining hall for a snack and chance to meet one another. At 11 o'clock, the kitchen help determined that cheese and cracker time was up and indicated everyone should leave by turning the lights off, although everyone wasn't ready to go yet.

I back the bike out of the van, park it along side and go to bed.

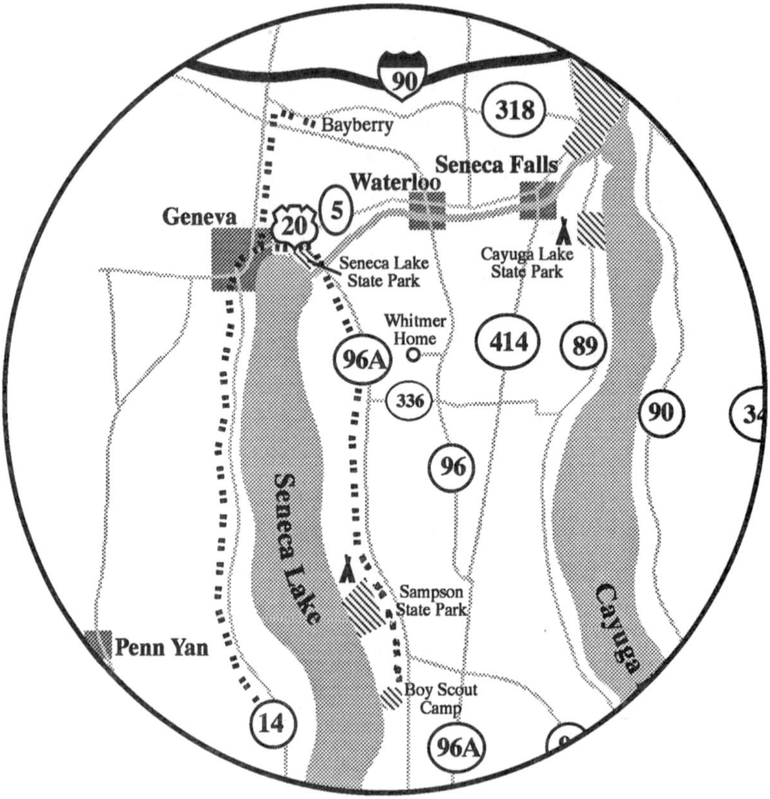
90
318
Bayberry
Seneca Falls
Waterloo
5
Geneva
20
Seneca Lake
State Park
Cayuga Lake
State Park
Whitmer
Home
96A
414
89
336
90
96
Seneca Lake
Sampson
State Park
Cayuga
Penn Yan
Boy Scout
Camp
14
96A

Fog & Bog

FOG & BOG

The earth is the Lord's and all that is in it,
the world and those who dwell therein.
For it was he who founded it upon the seas
and planted it firm upon the waters beneath.
Psalm 24 vs 1 & 2

This morning hardly seems like morning because the predicted rain caused a heavy grey damp fog to envelope and hide familiar landmarks. The bugle call to rise is muffled and the direction of the sound hard to pinpoint. By the time the breakfast call is blasted from the speakers on the roof of the mess hall, the fog has lifted just enough to see where I am walking.

This being the last day of camp, the muted breakfast noises are unenthusiastic and almost everyone looks like they would have rather stayed in bed. There are all combinations of breakfast eaters and I shudder at the probable behavior of Scouts who eat orange juice, sugar coated donuts and sugar coated cereal. After a couple of sleepy camp songs, announcements include admonishments to do last minute paperwork on merit badges and clean up campsites, and naming the finalists for the waterfront championship, the subdued Scouts are dismissed.

The brave reluctant participants assemble, shivering in their bathing suits, at the lakefront dock for the tug-of-war and canoe transfer event. The boy's movements are stiff as they get ready to brave the water.

The first tug-of-war takes several minutes to organize and fill in the vacancies left by the boys who refused the opportunity to be dunked in the water. Much to the dismay of the team in the lead they have to restart the contest because their rope is too long and their canoe runs into the dock of cheering spectators.

Even paddling on both sides of the canoe by so many boys is difficult and soon the boys begin to get tired. Once a canoe starts swinging on the rope the paddling becomes irregular. The trailing canoe leans, letting the water slip over the gunwale which further disrupts the paddling. In the effort to keep the canoe upright, they paddle harder on the invading water side, which lets more water in, then quickly the water is up to their waists and the game is over.

The canoe transfer consists of lashing two boards that hold the canoes about five feet apart, then holding the raft to keep it from floating out into the lake. On the whistle, the Scouts more or less in unison move ahead, crawl over the board to the other canoe, and take a place there. Meanwhile the other team is also crawling over the other board. The team that completes the transfer first wins. No one fell into the water because of their bobbing ride on the waves, but some got slivers in their knees from the boards.

Getting the canoes back to shore meant some had to jump into the water to help push the awkward raft back for the next teams. When the winners are announced the cheering is brief because the boys are halfway back to their campsites to get into warm clothes.

By the time the final inspection of the campsite is made, the sun is shining weakly. I wonder what the spirits of the Iroquois Conclave, held not far from here would think of today's competition; or how the Scouts would react if they suddenly found themselves in the Pleistocene era face to face with a mastodon claiming the camp as his.

With no more activities to prolong the stay, the van is packed with sleeping bags, wet bathing suits, muddy clothes, two tired Scouts and a Scoutmaster. My personal shelter transformed into a bus heads north on Route 96A toward Geneva.

First stop is for ice cream to ward off hunger for a little while. We go past Rose Hill Mansion to where 96A ends where it meets 5 & 20, and turn toward Geneva.

At the tip of the lake not far from the Seneca Canal is Seneca Lake State Park. There is a large marina and boat launch site, a large swimming beach, large lawns and fields. The fields are used by Hobart and William Smith Colleges for soccer and lacrosse practice in the fall and kite flying and baseball in the spring. It is an ideal place to fly kites because there are few trees, no wires and usually a good wind off the lake. There are also walks along the lake for hikers and bicycle riding. When strong south winds roar up the lake, waves lash the breakwall with hurricane-like fury, especially if the water is high. The old road ran along the edge of the water and on windy days you could have the car washed by the time you got around the end of the lake.

In 1835 Mr. Johnson from Scotland bought a farm a short distance south of the Seneca Outlet, but it was wet land. He remembered his grandfather in Scotland and how he had buried tile to drain the water off his field. When Mr. Johnson ordered the tile, they thought he was crazy. However when the other farmers saw his success, they borrowed his ideas and that is how tiling the fields first came to the Finger Lakes and made the land more productive.

At the tip of the lake closer to the city of Geneva is a new brick building overlooking the water. It is the Geneva Chamber of Commerce and it has all kinds of information on this area, New York State, Pennsylvania and Canada. The Chamber provides a meeting place for many local organizations and is the headquarters for the Annual Memorial Day National Lake Trout Fishing Derby. The contest draws people from all over to win one of the several prizes for the biggest trout caught by different age categories.

There is a boat ramp, picnic area, place to fish from the shore and an expansive view of the lake toward Watkins. A four-lane highway, built on fill, has long-since replaced the road on the lakes edge, and recently the shorefront has been earmarked for extensive lakeside development. Bickering over the shape and cost of the changes have stalled matters and the new Chamber building is the most radical change that has been made so far. Should local residents who oppose development lose their battle, proposed condominiums and hotels could dramatically change things.

We turn and go north on Route 14 toward the Thruway. Route 14 goes through part of the business district and straight to Sodus Point on Ontario Lake. We turn right on 318 about opposite the entrance to the Thruway and five miles down the road is Junius Ponds and the Bayberry Nature Center operated by the Girl Scouts.

The ponds at the Nature Center are unique. They are left over from glacial times and have fragile ecosystems not found elsewhere, including a bog. A bog is a deep water-filled hole with a thick layer of sphagnum moss, so thick and grown together it forms a cover. The water is trapped in the hole and because water doesn't flow in or out, there is little oxygen and so no algae or animal life. Because it is sterile, any hapless intruders who drowns, or pollen grains that fall in, remain intact. History can be read by

taking core samples from the bottom.

Specially adapted plants grow here as the gradual growth of the sphagnum moss is eventually thick enough to support waist high plants. Where the moss is thick it can be walked on. Jumping on it produces waves and quaking. It is a strange sensation to see the ground rippling. Whatever nutrients are available become locked up in the plants, making annual growth very slow. Small maples around the edges of the bog that look like saplings may be fifteen years old or more. One of nature's methods of compensating the plants for lack of nutrients is to make insect eating plants like the pitcher plant, the honey dew, or venus fly trap that bring nutrients in from other places.

The sundew plant has a tall slender stalk of white flowers and paddle-like leaves that exude a sticky dew-like substance that holds the inquisitive insects and digests out the nutrients.

The picher plant grows a trumpet-like trap, that has inviting juices at the bottom.Tiny slippery hairs facing downward allow the insect to go down but not back up. The insect finally gets into the juices at the bottom of the horn and is digested.

Other plants like the leather leaf, which is an evergreen, have other characteristics that help it survive. Its leaves are such that it prevents evaporation of water and nutrients.

Years of growth by the sphagnum moss, which is mined in Canada and called peat, ever so slowly fills in the bogs. There are stories of bandits purposely leading a posse into a bottomless bog at night to lose them in its depths and of robbers hiding their treasure in the water by hanging it on a rope and dangling it in the bog water.

Bayberry has trail areas set aside for Project Adventure and an assortment of other programs for adults and children. The reason for our visit was to show my husband the way their zip line is constructed so they could build one for the Boy Scouts. The zip line, one station in the Project Adventure Series, manned by trained volunteers, is a long cable attached to trees, over a stream or just down hill. With a mountain climbing harness and a safety line on, a metal loop is attached to a pulley that runs on the cable. The person jumps off a platform or the edge of the hill and slides down the cable to the far side, where there is someone to assist in unhooking from the cable.

Earlier in the year I had gone with a class of fifth-graders and participated in most of the first set of activities. The goals of Project Adventure are to develop self-confidence and mutual responsibility. It is also a good group-building activity.

After being fitted with a harness and helmet, I - who do not like to go beyond the first rung of a ladder - had to climb up a whole ten feet and get onto a postage-stamp size platform. Then the person on the platform is coached by another volunteer worker to jump into space. Palms wet with fear I HAD to show the class that if I could do it, so could they. My ride would have lasted longer if I had pulled my feet up so they hadn't dragged on the ground.

After making the measurements for constructing a zip line and feeding the mosquitos, we headed home, south on Route 14, but not without stopping at one of the many yard sales.

Practically every day of the week and especially on the weekends there are countless yard and garage sales where all kinds of treasure can be bought for bargain prices. The sales are held from the first warm weekends after Easter until Halloween. I'm not sure how all the quaint Antique shops in the area are affected; the sales may give them more opportunities to buy valuable pieces, which they in turn sell at one of the many auctions that seem to be held every weekend too.

Back through Geneva's business district and then down the shady tree lined street we pass older mansions turned into the fraternity and sorority houses of Hobart and William Smith Colleges. Another former home of the well-to-do is now the Geneva Historical Society in the Prouty-Chew House built in 1825.

Geneva was the first white settlement in the Genesee Country except for Jemima Wilkinson who settled the first time down the lake near Dresden. Geneva was a thriving cross roads of commerce and was the largest Indian Trading Center up to 1810. In 1790 at a cost of $2,300 the sailing sloop *Alexander* was launched. It served the settlements around the lake and delivered the mail. The first steamboat on the lake was the Seneca Chief in 1820. It burned 40 cords of wood to power the round trip from Geneva to Watkins.

Before the Erie Canal, the produce of the fields and orchards was made into whiskey or brandy via one of the 13 distilleries in Geneva because there was no way to ship bulk items.

Once the canal was opened, the Finger Lakes became the breadbasket of New York City, then became less important as railroads,-opened up the west. In 1878 coal was being shipped to New York City from Pennsylvania by way of Seneca Lake and the Erie Canal.

When visiting Geneva today, it's hard to believe that the beautiful city was a treeless plain in the early 1800's. First it was cleared for farming, then the remaining wood was used for buildings and for fuel. When the land gave out, many of the people moved west looking for good land.

In 1849 the Geneva Medical College was the first to grant a medical degree to a woman in America, Elisabeth Blackwell. In 1872 the College moved to Syracuse and became part of Syracuse University.

On the outskirts of Geneva are two rolling golf courses with a scenic view of Seneca Lake. The Finger Lakes has about 24 well kept courses including the one in Corning where the LPGA is held. For those who prefer a shorter round, there are many miniature golf courses too.

South of Geneva is a small bay called Glass Factory Bay. A factory was built to manufacture window panes for the fast growing state. When the canal was completed, the factory was too far away from the main shipping path and, having other difficulties, was closed. Later, a colored glass factory was opened but that didn't do well either and was abandoned in 1847. The only visible remains of the settlement are a small school house turned into a home and some street signs. It is now known for the good seasonal fishing in the bay.

Out from shore in 115 feet of water in Glass Factory Bay are the intact remains of a canal boat. Scuba divers from diving clubs all over, dive regularly in the Finger Lakes on historic and interesting wrecks. The largest wreck is in 65 feet of water off Severne

Point seven miles south of Dresden and opposite the closed Morton Salt Mines.

At night in the early spring along the western shore of Seneca Lake in Kashong Creek (and many other streams that feed the Finger Lakes) are hip-booted fishermen with bright lanterns scooping up little fish called smelt. The hardy souls brave the icy water late at night to intercept a few smelt that are literally a drop in the bucket of all the smelt that swim upstream to spawn. The little fish, beheaded and gutted, dipped in batter and deep fried, rate as high as any sea food anywhere.

The Kashong Creek ceases to flow some summers. Long ago it was continuously fed by a large watershed of forest, now most of the land is tilled. Before white man built dams and mills on the fast flowing stream there was a good size Indian settlement here. Besides the fish there were game, fruit, berries and a deposit of flint and the Native Americans raised corn and squash and maintained orchards. Spring floods washed the collected garbage into the lake so they wouldn't have to move to get away from it.

There were 22 bark huts here when Sullivan and Clinton destroyed the settlement in 1779. Graves of people who lived here more than 1500 years ago have been found in the valley and on the surrounding banks. Now because the water doesn't flow year round, bushes and shrubs have grown into the stream bed.

Kashong is world famous for the fossils exposed by the water. Fossils from the Devonian period are scattered along the creek bed. You experience a special feeling when you hit a rock, it splits, and for the first time, human eyes see the fossil remains of an ancient plant or animal over 350 million years old.

Fossil hunting is allowed with permission from the landowner, Mark Powers, who lives in one of the first houses built in this area. It is on the south crest of the bank, back from the main highway. Indian spirits spoke to Mr. Powers and he wrote a book on the history of the glen and the surrounding area called *Kashong: A History From the Ancient to the Modern*.

***

The settlement of the Public Universal Friend, established by the colorful Jemima Wilkinson, along the Keuka Outlet near the town of Dresden, had more people in 1790 than Geneva. She moved the settlement to Guyanoga Valley north of the western arm of Keuka Lake when her title to the land was questioned because of an error in an early survey. The erroneous survey caused many probelms in the area and Pre-Emption Road got its name because it follows the lines of a revised survey which pre-empted the original. The Outlet settlement had water power; something Geneva didn't have. In 1820 there were 27 mills and several distilleries along the stream that drained Keuka into Seneca.

Keuka Outlet's eight mile natural outflow drops 270 feet. The Crooked Lake Canal was built in 1833, with 28 locks, in spite of an engineer's report that it would not be economical. In 1873 it was abandoned and in 1884 the Fall Creek Railroad was built over part of the Canal.

The railroad was abandoned when hurricane Agnes washed out portions of the track in 1972. The railroad right of way was bought by Yates County and made into a linear park, winding through the picturesque historical gorge. Trail Guides are available from the Yates County Historical Society located in the Oliver House in Penn Yan, the Public Library and many of the stores.

At the mouth of the Outlet on Keuka Lake, is the town of Penn Yan, which stands for Pennsylvania Yankee. It is home of the Finger Lakes Association, which promotes tourism and business opportunities in the Finger Lakes. Traveling down main street you can smell the appetizing aroma from the worlds largest buckwheat mill. Birkett Mills made local history (and the Guinness Book of Records) with the worlds largest Buckwheat Pancake. The massive flapjack was created at the First Annual Buckwheat Festival in 1987. The two day September celebration was such a success they are making it bigger and better each year with famous entertainers, buckwheat products, arts, crafts and contests.

The smallness of the stream should not be taken lightly because there is a fast current in spite of its size. It would be a good idea to walk the trail before attempting to canoe the rocky stream. There are two portages, around Seneca Mills Falls and Cascade Mills. With the amount of land planted there is little area to hold the rain water, so a heavy rain raises the level quickly turning the usually serene water to a twisting white-water for an experienced canoeist only.

Several years ago we decided to canoe down the Outlet, in spite of the water being low. We had to let the canoe down with a rope in several places and never went the entire length.

Even with the variable water levels there is the possibility a seasonal hydroelectric power plant will be built. There was a water power plant once but it was replaced by a coal fired electric plant built in Dresden. Most of the land along the Outlet is owned by NYSG&E company and they have been helpful with the development of the Outlet Trail.

Now that the waste treatment plant for Penn Yan is operating, the stones below the discharge should not be as slippery as when we canoed it. Much of the garbage and natural debris has been cleared from along the water way. Hurricane Agnes raised the level of Seneca Lake 4 feet (a mind boggling amount of water for a lake nearly 40 miles long) causing much erosion of the Outlet banks.

Now there is rip-rap where erosion is most likely.

When the Outlet is full, it thunders over Seneca Mills Falls and before the chutes were bricked up you could feel the ground vibrate from the power of the falling water.

Local history is not confined to the mills and locks. Dresden, incorporated in 1867, enjoyed prosperity until about 1870 when many fires destroyed its businesses and they were not rebuilt. The abandonment of the Canal didn't help Dresden either. Later it became a railroad depot but never regained the prosperity of olden times.

Dresden people view having the birthplace of the once popular orator, Robert Ingersoll in their town with mixed feelings. Born in 1833, the son of a Congregational minister, Ingersoll practiced and preached upright behavior but not the trappings of various religions. His house has undergone several remodelings and is presently being restored to serve as a museum. Robert was a friend of Mark Twain who lived and is buried in Elmira, about thirty miles south of Dresden. Twain wrote *Tom Sawyer, Adventures of Huckleberry Finn* and other books in an octagonal study at Quarry Farm.

Elmira is popular for its re-enactments of the Civil War battles. The National Soaring Museum, located nearby at Harris Hill is where, for a small fee, you can soar and ride the thermals with the hawks and see the beauty of the Central Finger Lakes as they see it.

The Seneca Indian rite of Thanksgiving for a bountiful harvest is still practiced around Keuka Lake on Labor Day. The festival of lights or Ring of Fire once celebrated with bonfires is now celebrated with flares, all lit at the same time, outlining Keuka at night and creating a large polluting smoke cloud.

Besides exciting winter ice boating and summer sailing, Penn Yan has indirectly influenced other sports. In 1891 James Naismith was asked to devise a game for a school that could be played indoors during the winter season. It happened that a Penn Yan man, Edson Potter was in Connecticut at the time trying to sell Penn Yan made peach baskets. James bought two of the baskets and basketball was born. At first it was played with the bottoms left intact and then evolved to the string baskets of today. At the southern end of Keuka Lake in Hammondsport is the Glenn Curtiss Aviation Museum. The first flying boat and other air craft firsts took place on the quiet waters of Keuka Lake.

Keuka, Seneca and Cayuga Lakes have sheer cliffs, gorges and gullies which make it impossible to have a road all the way around the lake near the water. The natural islands created by the gullies have kept some areas undeveloped and left places where wildlife is undisturbed. So, mixed with farms and cottages is an abundance of wildlife that might not have been left if the lake shores were level. These pockets of wildlife are part of the treasure of this region.

Country people are more aware that their existence is tied to the land and their care of it. It never ceases to amaze me how people move to the country for all its beauty, and then proceed to erect a building and immediately mow down all the "weeds" to make a large flat barren lawn. Destroying habitat and thereby killing wildlife, they use nonrenewable resources to keep it mowed. A particular area can only support so much wildlife and the overflow or intruding wildlife doesn't have much chance of survival. Planting for wildlife actually costs less to maintain than an expensive lawn.

***

Home once again, we unload the van and start the task of putting things back in order and washing clothes. After bringing some semblance of order to the chaos I am drawn to a solitary late evening hike to the lake to muse on my Retreat.

My black shadow and I walk to the edge of the rippling silver wedge of moonlight in the early almost day-bright moonlight night. The large, late rising, eye-level moon has created a silver road to the far off shore. Miniature foaming waves tickle the worn snuggled stones, telling indiscernible stories to the moon-basking beach spirits.

Short dark sentinel pilings, remainders of a long ago busy grape dock pierce the waves, but are unable to halt the marching army. In front, not far from shore, a children's island of heaped up stones and imaginative plays in the summer sunshine is being reclaimed by the persistent waves. Swirling breezes, alternately warm from the land and cool from the water, flap our light jackets open. Only a few of the brave bright stars dare to shine when Mr. Moon is full on.

***

Crickets, katydids and peepers gossip their calls in the dark lunar shadows of the woods.

Into the noises of lapping waves, dancing light and creature chorus a large flapping shadow glides and splashes into the twinkling silver highway. The dark shadow mixes and blends with the rearing waves and remains motionless in the moving light.

In between waves, and moonbeam flashes, I can make out an oval body on chopstick legs with a snake like neck ending in a spear. Not twenty feet away, merging and blending with the traveling waves, a great blue heron stalks its prey. How did he know how deep it was right here and how far out to go?

Freeze! Stay still and see what happens next! Slowly the long neck extends, the head cranes forward looking for silver flashes above the stones. Nothing, nothing and nothing. A slow single deliberate ever so slow step. One step, two steps, then turn around and go back again. Waves straining to slap the barely existing shadow's feather bottom. Take a break, flap the wings lightly on the water, quick shower and preen to unlock stiff legs and hunt again.

***

Hardly breathe, don't dare move, pretend to be a silver moonlit tree.

***

Poor fishing tonight. Shadows of waves and moonlight allow the hunted to see the patient hunter. More than 80 miles of shore to patrol and the heron has chosen to hunt these favored five moon-glowing yards. Back and forth slowly stalking. With each step of the hunter it's more difficult for me to hold still. Our acquaintance grows and the moon road shrinks away as the moon climbs higher.

Slowly, but not slow enough, I move to close the jacket against the cool breeze. The alert heron gives the alarm, "frahnk", flaps noisily into the air and glides toward the shore beyond the sentinel pilings.

Man plans his journey by his own wits,
but it is the Lord who guides his steps.
Proverbs 16 vs 9

INFORMATION & RESOURCES

MAPS

New York State Atlas & Gazetteer - DeLorme Mapping Company, P.O. Box 298, Freeport, Maine 04032 (207) 865-4171

Visual Encyclopedia - The Finger Lakes Region of New York State. Marshall Penn-York Co. Inc., 538 Erie Blvd. W., Syracuse, NY 13204 Tel.(315) 422-2162

New York State Finger Lakes Bicycle Touring Map, Office of Parks Recreation and Historic Preservation, Base Map 1980, Box 283, R.D. #3, Trumansburg, NY 14886-0721 Tel.(607) 387-7041

Finger Lakes Trail Conference, P.O. Box 18048, Rochester, NY 14618

Finger Lakes Association, 309 Lake Street, Penn Yan, NY 14527 - $1.75, ask for MAP. All roads in the fourteen county region. Also have a booklet covering places to stay, things to do, a superb guide to the Finger Lakes area.

COUNTY MAPS - *Write Department of Highways*

Cayuga County - Auburn, NY 13021
Chemung County - Horseheads, NY 14845
Cortland County - Cortland, NY 13045
Monroe County - Rochester/Monroe County Visitors Bureau, Rochester, NY 14604
Ontario County - Canandaigua, NY 14424
Schuyler County - Watkins Glen, NY 14891
Seneca County - Waterloo, NY 13165
Tompkins County - Ithaca, NY 14850
Wayne County - Lyons, NY 14489
Yates County - Penn Yan, NY 14527

STARTER INFORMATION -

Guide to NY State's Outdoors, office of Parks, Recreation and Historic Preservation, Empire State Plaza, Albany, NY 12238
Department of Environmental Conservation, 50 Wolf Road, Albany, NY 12233

Finger Lakes State Parks, Recreation and Historic Preservation Region, Box 283, RD #3, Trumansburg, NY 14886-0721. Tel.(607) 387-7401
Finger Lakes Association, 309 Lake Street, Penn Yan, NY 14527 Tel.(315) 536-7488
Ch. of Comm. of Auburn and Cayuga County, 144 Genesee St. Auburn, NY 13021 Tel.(315) 252-7291
Ch. of Comm., P.O. Box 317, Fair Haven, NY 13064
Canandaigua Ch. of Comm., 3210 Eastern Blvd., Canandaigua NY 14424
Geneva Ch. of Comm., Routes 5 & 20, Geneva, NY 14456
Seneca County Ch. of Comm., 2022 Routes 5 & 20 West Seneca Falls, NY 13148 Tel.(315) 568-5505
The Schuyler County Ch. of Comm., 100 North Franklin Street Watkins Glen, NY 14891 Tel.(607) 535-4300
Greater Bath Area Ch. of Comm., 21 Liberty Street, Bath, NY 14810
Tompkins County Ch. of Comm., 122 W. Court St., Ithaca, NY 15841 Tel.(607) 243-7080
Wayne County Public Information Office, Dept 3AA, 21 Butternut Street, Lyons, NY 14489 Tel.(315) 946-6191
Penn Yan Ch. of Comm., PO Box 432, 100 Main Street, Penn Yan, NY 14527

BICYCLING

Freewheeling Adventures, 84 Duran Drive, Rochester, NY 14622 Tel.(716) 323-2567

HIKING

Finger Lakes Trail Conference, P.O. Box 18048, Rochester, NY 14618

FISHING

Region 7 Fishing Hotline (607) 753-1551) Cayuga Lake east DEC Office PO Box 1169, Cortland N.Y. 13040 Tel.(607) 753-3095

Region 8 DEC (Seneca Lake and west) 6274 E. Avon-Lima Road, Avon, NY 14414 Tel.(716) 226-2466